D0909597

BERKELEY'S IMMATERIALISM

Berkeley's Immaterialism

A Commentary on his "A Treatise Concerning
the Principles of Human Knowledge"

A. A. Luce M.C. D.D. Litt.D.

*Berkeley Professor of Metaphysics
in the University of Dublin*

NEW YORK / RUSSELL & RUSSELL

FIRST PUBLISHED IN 1945 BY THOMAS NELSON & SONS LTD.

REISSUED, 1968, BY RUSSELL & RUSSELL

A DIVISION OF ATHENEUM HOUSE, INC.

BY ARRANGEMENT WITH

THOMAS NELSON & SONS LTD., LONDON

L: C. CATALOG CARD NO: 68-25034

PRINTED IN THE UNITED STATES OF AMERICA

PREFACE (1968)

READERS who verify quotations are asked to note that quotations from Berkeley's *Principles* throughout this book are taken, as is stated on page 10, from the text of the first edition (1710, ed. T. E. Jessop, 1937). No scholarly text of the second edition (1734) was available when my book went first to press. Jessop's text of the second edition is now available in our edition of the *Works*, vol. II. I have *checked ad hoc* all the quotations from the *Principles* that occur in the following pages, and can assure the reader that the textual differences in the two editions (*e.g. intirely* for *entirely*) are negligible, so far as concerns my argument. Even the omission of the vague word 'notions' from section 25 (quoted below p. 93, line 2) is not significant *there*.

The biographical *Introduction* opened out and eventually became my *Life of George Berkeley*.

Berkeley's answer (*Princ.* 45-48) to the crucial Objection IV on the alleged intermittent existence of his ideas of sense is, I think, correctly analysed and stated below (pp. 120-25); but I give it more fully and clearly in my *The Dialectic of Immaterialism*, London, 1963 (pp. 32-38).

Trinity College,   A. A. Luce
Dublin
January, 1968

PREFACE

BERKELEY is a clear writer, but his terminology leaves him peculiarly open to misunderstanding, and he needs an interpreter to-day. I have tried to give here a faithful and documented interpretation of his argument for immaterialism set forth in his *Principles of Human Knowledge*.

My documentation is in the design and fabric of the book rather than in its footnotes. From Chapter II onwards, as the chapter headings show, I have worked systematically through the text of the *Principles*, handling the sections substantially in their order and following the natural articulations of the work. Nothing of present-day importance has been omitted, I think, but I have not dwelt on details nor lingered on points of merely historical interest. I have proportioned my treatment to the weight of Berkeley's argument, not to its length, and therefore the first thirty-three sections receive the lion's share of attention and space ; for they contain practically the whole of the direct argument. I am not saying that the rest of the book is unimportant ; sections 34 to 84 answer objections, sections 85 to 156 draw consequences, but these sections make scarcely any positive contribution to the essence of the case for immaterialism, which is virtually complete by section 33.

My theme is Berkeley's refutation of material substance, and I have kept it in view strictly and steadily throughout, subordinating the other parts and aspects of the Berkeleian philosophy, which are only of incidental importance to-day. For similar reasons I have confined myself to the *Principles* and have referred to Berkeley's other works as little as possible. Berkeley's gift to world thought was, and is, his immaterialism, and he placed it entire in one casket, the *Principles*. He published a preparatory study and several sequels, but he published no substitute for the *Principles* ; even the *Three Dialogues* cannot take its place. The mature student should read the *Essay on Vision*, both sets of dialogues, the *De Motu*, the *Siris*, and the minor works, but the novice should concentrate on the *Principles*, which offers a complete argument for immaterialism, appealing only to reason. I have read all Berkeley's other writings carefully, critically, and *ad hoc* ; I recognize their value, but I am convinced that they add nothing to the essential argument of the *Principles*, and take nothing from it. Master the *Principles*, and you have mastered Berkeley's immaterialism.

The term *Commentary* in the sub-title should be understood in a broad sense. The book is not a string of comments ; it is not overloaded with detailed references, and for the most part it can be read by him who runs. I wrote it with the *Principles* open and at hand, and it can be so read if desired ; but I am rather the expositor (to use an old term) than the commentator ; for I have aimed at giving an exposition, a free-hand, fighting exposition, of Berkeley's teaching about matter. I have not criticized that teaching here. I have no criticisms of it to make now ; my old criticisms of it glare and glower at me reproachfully from the margins of my well-thumbed textbooks. I am not prepared *jurare in verba magistri*, but I hold that Berkeley's immaterialism is sound commonsense, and is seen to be such when it is cleared of misunderstandings and correctly presented.

We have had new light on Berkeley lately. Since Fraser's day many new Berkeley letters have been published (nearly one hundred by Rand, some forty by me) ; we have new sermons of his, too, and *miscellanea*. But the chief new document is that pair of notebooks which Fraser found and published seventy years ago under the title *Commonplace Book of Occasional Metaphysical Thoughts*, and which I have re-named *Philosophical Commentaries* in my edition (1944). From the point of view of exact scholarship this is a new document to-day. Under its old name it has been known to the philosophical world for two generations, but no intelligent handling of it was possible till recently. Fraser could not make head or tail of it (as his name for it confesses) ; and no wonder, for he thought the head the tail, and the tail the head, and published it all topsy-turvy. Dr. G. A. Johnston's edition (1930) marked a big step in the right direction, but its text is inaccurate ; it has not completely straightened out Fraser's initial mistake about the structure, and it has perpetuated mistaken views about the general character of the work and its date. Now, however, the structure, date, and purpose of the work have been determined, and a correct text published, and in the light of this new-old document, often cited in the following pages, the key doctrines of the *Principles* can be read more clearly and interpreted more precisely than has hitherto been possible. We are now in a position to reject several popular misconceptions of Berkeley's teaching, as well as those grave misrepresentations of it which are becoming stereotyped in our textbooks.

A poet's mind is a representative mind, and I need not apologize for referring here to the recently published Diary (1930) of W. B. Yeats (I owe the facts to Dr. A. N. Jeffares) which, read along with his Introduction to *Bishop Berkeley* (J. M. Hone and M. M. Rossi), illustrates and exemplifies the general interest in Berkeley, the widespread uncertainty as to what he taught, and the clash of opinion about him.

Yeats in later life came under the spell of Berkeley, and fell in love with him, but appears to have been puzzled and perplexed about him. What manner of man was Berkeley ? What did he really teach ? Failing to find satisfactory answers, the poet projected his own questionings, it would seem, into the actual experience of the philosopher. He found, or thought he found, *two* Berkeleys. Berkeley was " idealist and realist alike " ; Berkeley " wore a mask " ; " in the Commonplace Book alone is Berkeley always sincere . . . Berkeley the bishop was a humbug."

These *obiter dicta* are (no disrespect to the poet is intended) nonsense, charming inconsequent nonsense, sparkles of poetic fancy without foundation in fact. There was only one George Berkeley in actual life ; he never wore a mask, and he was transparently honest and single-minded. Yeats was quite wrong about his " sage and saint," but he has said some true things, and said them finely, about " that fierce young man " in whom his soul delighted ; and the struggle in the poet's mind about him mirrors a wider dialectic, the perennial struggle in the public mind between the true Berkeley and the false.

Yeats met the true Berkeley in the pages of " the Commonplace Book with its snorts of defiance " ; the poet revelled in those notebooks, and from them he learned the simple truth which he expressed in the words, " Descartes, Locke, and Newton, took away the world . . . Berkeley restored the world. Berkeley has brought back to us the world that only exists because it shines and sounds." The false Berkeley Yeats knew, as we all do, by hearsay ; it is the Berkeley of legend and textbook tradition ; it is the long-haired, languishing visionary depicted in that mural decoration which does duty as " portrait of Berkeley " in the Examination Hall of his College ; it is, in Yeats' words, the

> God-appointed Berkeley that proved all things a dream
>> That this pragmatical preposterous pig of a world,
>> Its farrow that so solid seem,
> Must vanish on the instant if the mind but change its theme.

The Berkeley of those lines is not the true Berkeley, not the Berkeley Yeats really loved ; for the " Berkeley that proved all things a dream " filled no notebooks, published no philosophy, never existed in the flesh. He exists only in the minds of critics and scoffers, and of those who never read the *Principles* but glean their scraps of knowledge about it from criticisms and witticisms.

To destroy that pseudo-Berkeley, and to restore to his rightful place the real Berkeley who proved the world *no* dream are the master aims of this book, as they have been the main motives of my philosophical studies for some years past.

My colleague, Mr. F. La T. Godfrey, has very kindly read the work in manuscript, and has made valuable criticisms and suggestions.

A. A. LUCE

TRINITY COLLEGE
DUBLIN, *March 1945*

CONTENTS

§§ refer to sections of Berkeley's *Principles*

LIST OF ABBREVIATIONS

INTRODUCTION

BERKELEY lived an active, many-sided life, was much in the public eye, and wrote on many things besides philosophy. A full-length biography and an adequate account of his writings would be out of place here, but I must say something about his life and works in order to dispel the legends which have gathered round his name. I wish to show him as a normal man of flesh and blood in constant and fruitful touch with the real world, and I must draw in some detail the background of his *Principles*. Thanks to the happy accident of the survival of certain documents, a great deal of information is available about the genesis of Berkeley's masterpiece, and that information lends strong support to the commonsense interpretation of the work which I shall advance in the following chapters.

George Berkeley, son of William Berkeley of Thomastown, Co. Kilkenny, was born at Kilkenny [1] on the 12th of March 1685. At the age of eleven he was entered at Kilkenny College, the school of Swift, Congreve, Admiral Beatty, and many other eminent men. He spent four years there, and then passed on to Trinity College, Dublin, where he matriculated on the 21st of March 1700. The university was his home or headquarters for

[1] The Trinity College Entrance Book has the entry which must have come from Berkeley himself, " natus Kilkenniae Ibi educatus sub Dre Hinton." The statement in Stock's *Life* that he was born " at Kilcrin near Thomastown " represents a conflation, I think, of two facts which seem to me established, (a) that he was born at Kilcrene, a townland a mile or two from Kilkenny city, which still gives its name to more than one residence, and (b) that he was brought up at or near Dysart Castle, now in ruins, on the river Nore about two miles from Thomastown ; see Appendix to my article, *Proc. R. I. Acad.*, vol. xlviii., C. 7.

twenty-four years.   For the first part of that period he was resident, as student, scholar, and fellow ; he then went away on leave of absence for eight and a half years, retaining his fellowship ; he returned in September 1721, and took his part in the work of the college till his appointment as Dean of Derry in May 1724.

His undergraduate course consisted of mathematics, languages (Latin and Greek, with some French and Hebrew), and philosophy, and his all-round proficiency is shown by the fact that before he was twenty he had written a series of mathematical tracts in good Latin, publishing them in 1707 under the titles *Arithmetica* . . . and *Miscellanea mathematica*. . . . Elected scholar of the House in 1702, he graduated B.A. in the spring of 1704. In the autumn of 1706 a fellowship fell vacant, and after competing successfully at the statutory fellowship examination, he was elected fellow on the 9th of June 1707.   He took Holy Orders, as required by the statutes, and for the next five or six years he was occupied with the routine work of the college and with his own writing.

The crisis of his intellectual life occurred probably soon after his graduation.   Some time before the end of 1706 the notion of immaterialism must have come to him.   *How* it came we cannot say precisely.   The spirit of " the Enlightenment " would dispose a bold young thinker who, on his own statement, was " distrustful[1] at 8 years old " to question the traditional account of sense perception, which is anything but " clear and distinct." The two specific influences helping to mould his thought in its plastic period were Locke's *Essay* and the Cartesian philosophy in its Malebranchian form, and Berkeley seems

---

[1] " sceptical," *prima manu* ; *PC* 266. This interesting little note shows, when taken with the previous entry, that Berkeley was asking himself, How did I come to think of immaterialism ?

to have regarded [1] both Locke and Malebranche as con-
tributors to the argument for immaterialism.

Locke's *Essay* was on the Dublin curriculum within
two years of its publication. Owing to the influence of
Locke's friend, Molyneux, it had an immediate effect on
Irish thought. It was taught, but taught critically, by
Peter Browne, author of *The Procedure, Extent, and Limits
of Human Understanding* (1728), and *Things Divine and
Supernatural Conceived by Analogy . . .* (1733), who was
Provost when Berkeley was a student, and it was clearly
the basis of Berkeley's philosophical education. Could
Berkeley have learned immaterialism from it ? If he did
so, it must have been by reaction and on the rebound.
Locke was a firm believer in matter, and a strong champion of the claim of solidity to be a characteristic quality
of matter ; his theory of perception is thoroughly matterist.
Immaterialism would not grow naturally from such a soil.
If Locke did provoke Berkeley to deny matter, he did so,
not by his positive instruction, but negatively by exempli-
fying the sceptical tendencies latent in representationism.
Locke, it is true, placed the secondary qualities in the
mind ; but so did the Cartesians and all the " moderns " ;
and that line of argument, though it could be used *ad
hominem* by the immaterialist up to a point, is in its broader
implications an argument *for* matter and not against it, as
Berkeley found.[2] Locke's ideism, his " new way of
ideas," is often regarded as having led Berkeley to call
things of sense " ideas." There may be a grain of truth
in that contention, but it certainly does not take us to the
source of Berkeley's immaterialism. Berkeley was an
immaterialist long before he adopted the term *idea* for
the immediate object of sense.[3] He was very slow to

[1] See *PC* 265–66. Stock's *Life* names both Locke and Malebranche
in this connection.   [2] *Princ.* § 15.   [2] *PC* 115, 153 ; see my notes *ib.*

adopt this term, and his idea of sense differs *toto coelo* from that of Locke, and Berkeley knew it. The term used is the same, but the one idea is a representation, the other a presentation. I think Locke here influenced Berkeley's technique and terminology but not his doctrine. Locke had popularized the term *idea* for the immediate object, and Berkeley could hardly avoid the term. In particular Locke's phrase " collection of ideas " had made it very easy for Berkeley to use the same phrase, though in a widely different sense[1]; but I do not see that Locke's *Essay per se* could teach any thinker to doubt or deny the existence of matter.

The opinion that Berkeley was a successor to Locke and learned immaterialism from the *Essay* is of recent growth. Berkeley's contemporaries thought of him rather as a disciple of Malebranche. I do not go that length ; for Berkeley was too independent a thinker to be any man's disciple, and himself says of Malebranche, " Upon the whole there are no principles more fundamentally opposite than his and mine." [2] But there is no doubt at all that Berkeley in his younger days was steeped in the *Recherche*. There he could have found, and I believe did find, a *positive* impulse towards immaterialism ; for Malebranche, while nominally retaining matter, builds without it, queries its existence in his well-known *Illustration* [3] (*excursus*) on " 'Tis very difficult to prove the existence of bodies," and advances such bad " proofs " of its existence that a child could see through them.

---

[1] See below, p. 41*ff.*

[2] *Three Dialogues*, ii *ad. med.* This passage was inserted in the third edition (1734) clearly in reply to criticism. In the first edition the connection (partial) with the doctrine of seeing all things in God is tacitly admitted, rather than denied. See my *Berkeley and Malebranche*, pp. 82–83.

[3] This *Illustration* is named in the *Commentaries* ; see Nos. 686, 800, with my notes.

In a sense it does not matter now who taught Berkeley to deny matter ; perhaps no man taught him. And yet the question of origin has its importance for exegesis and interpretation. Some modern misinterpretations of Berkeley's philosophy can be traced to the lengthening tradition of his sole dependence upon Locke, and can be obviated by a frank and balanced recognition of the influence of Malebranche. If the Berkeleian idea of sense be interpreted from the standpoint of Lockian " psychologism," *i.e.* if it be taken as a product of man's thinking, the Berkeleian philosophy, to my mind, is nonsense. But take the idea of sense as a sensible idea, as a sense datum given by God to man, *i.e.* reintegrate it in that vision of all things in God which was common to Berkeley and Malebranche, energize it, or rather activate it, with the causal power of the " One True Cause," taught by Malebranche and not by Locke, and it becomes the typical element of the world of sense, viewed as the scene of the immediate operation of the infinite Spirit, the expression of His power and wisdom. That was Berkeley's philosophy of the world. It is a reasonable view, leading to rational conceptions of God and the world and the relation between them.

Berkeley considered the *pros* and *cons* of immaterialism with great care ; we can be sure of that, because we have the two notebooks in which he did a great deal of the preliminary work. Fraser named these notebooks *Commonplace Book of Occasional Metaphysical Thoughts* ; that name is a bad name which has given the world a wrong impression of their nature and contents. I have renamed the work *Philosophical Commentaries*,[1] because the notebooks are, primarily and in the main, commentaries upon the arguments for immaterialism, written or unwritten, which

[1] I often abbreviate to *Commentaries*.

Berkeley was examining. The work throws a flood of
light upon the development [1] of Berkeley's thought in
those early days, and settles several disputed points in
the interpretation of his teaching. All should study it
who wish to see Berkeley's thought in the making.[2] I
must add a word of warning about the use of the notebooks. Berkeley did not intend them to be read by any
eye but his own, and we must not take everything he
writes in them as his settled opinion. It was for him
a period of intensive speculation and rapid intellectual
development. While he was making these entries he
changed his mind on several issues of first importance.
Random quotations, therefore, from the work can be
most misleading, and any use of it in argument ought to
be preceded by critical study with a view to sifting
Berkeley's passing notions or *ad interim* hypotheses from
his official tenets. The final views expressed in these
notebooks are, I think, in entire agreement with the
published doctrine of the *Principles*.

We pass on to the first of the great publications, *An
Essay towards a New Theory of Vision*, which, as the *Commentaries* shows, was on the stocks along with the *Principles*.
This book appeared in 1709, and reached a second edition
within a twelvemonth. To-day it is generally regarded
as inferior to the *Principles* (and I concur in that judgement),
but in the past it has been by far the more influential
of the two works. Berkeley in his lifetime was an accepted
authority on vision on the Continent as well as at home,
and before the end of the eighteenth century and well
into the nineteenth his psychology of vision was the
received account—and that at a time when his immaterial-

---

[1] No later development occurred ; see my " The Alleged Development of Berkeley's Philosophy " *Mind*, vol. lii, N.S., No. 206.

[2] In my edition (pp. 317–18) I have listed my " Key Doctrinal Notes."
These cover practically all the important points of interpretation or exegesis.

ism was, for the most part, regarded as a great man's folly.

The relation between the *Essay on Vision* and the *Principles* is subtle, complex, and paradoxical, but very instructive and interesting. The later book was the parent book. The *Essay* sprang from the *Principles* [1] and not *vice versa*. The *Essay* stands on its own feet, and yet prepares the way for the *Principles*. The two works are harmonious, and in sharp disagreement. The *Essay* was an *ad interim* work intended to be superseded by the *Principles* ; yet in the latter work Berkeley appeals to the former to support his case, while speaking of it as a work of limited scope with an argument of limited validity. The *Principles* contains Berkeley's full and final doctrine of immaterialism, and to it the *Essay* must give way where there is any conflict. Yet Berkeley would have his American converts read both works, and he sent them copies of both. Moreover he appended the *Essay* to his *Alciphron*, which was published twenty-two years after the *Principles*, following it up a year later with *The Theory of Vision . . . Vindicated and Explained*.

These paradoxes are in large measure resolved by considering the different parts, purposes, and aspects of the *Essay on Vision*. It was an independent work on optics, appealing to a wide public because of the wide use, then beginning to be made, of spectacles, microscopes, telescopes, and other optical instruments. It was a work on the psychology of vision, still quoted in text-books of psychology. It was also a work on metaphysics, and, as such, it had a double purpose. It was to serve as an instalment of immaterialism, revealing one-half of that creed and one-half only, acting, in effect, like the thin end of the wedge. Yet it was to establish a major prin-

[1] *Princ.* 43.

ciple of immaterialism, destined eventually to carry the whole position.

Let me develop the point.　As Berkeley worked out his " immaterial hypothesis " (*PC* 19), and attacked the matterist [1] conception of a world outside the range of mind, he was pulled up by the commonsense objection that we *see* the outside world and see it outside.　He set himself to answer that objection by determining precisely what takes place when a man sees, and he concludes that we *see*, not angles or matter, but modes of light and colour, and *infer* distance, magnitude, and situation on the basis of sensations such as eye strain and the confusion and faintness of the object.　He reached these results by placing the visible and the tangible in extremely sharp opposition. He calls them *heterogeneous*, meaning thereby not only that they are objects of specifically different senses, but that they differ generically, in nature, the visible being in the mind and the tangible not.　Thus Berkeley in his *Essay on Vision* brings the visible world into the mind, and leaves the tangible world outside, allowing his readers to assume, and in one or two passages almost suggesting, that the tangible world is the world of matter.　The first part of the thesis prepares the way for immaterialism, the second part bangs and bolts the door against it.

The *Principles* goes the whole way and reaches positions incompatible with those of the *Essay*.　When matter completely disappears, the visible and the tangible clearly possess the same metaphysical status.　If the visible is still the sign of the tangible, the tangible is equally the sign of the visible.　If the visible is in the mind, so too is the tangible. It becomes then a nice question as to how far they can be called heterogeneous ; and if their heterogeneity goes, is there any point in denying outness and distance ? [2]

[1] For my use of *matterist*, see p. 25*n*.　　[2] See pp. 119-20.

In these respects the outlook of the two books is very different, but there is one very important tenet in which they agree. Both books regard God as expressing Himself in objects of sense, which therefore constitute a language or set of symbols in which His existence and nature can be read. In the *Essay* the argument is restricted to the objects of sight which are said to " constitute the universal language of nature " (*TV* 147), but in the *Principles* (108*ff.*) all the objects of all the senses come under a similar designation.

The background of the *Principles* has thus been sketched. Its actual argument for immaterialism is discussed in detail in the following pages, and I need say nothing about it here. But there are some literary details which should be recorded. First, two manuscripts must be mentioned which are of interest and of some importance for comparative study. A draft of the Introduction is contained, *inter alia*, in Berkeley's notebook known as the Chapman MS.[1] It follows the main lines of the existing Introduction, but is much longer, and its text is closer to the corresponding entries in the *Commentaries*. Berkeley wrote it, or wrote it out, towards the end of 1708, beginning it on the 15th of November and finishing it on the 18th of December. Fraser printed it as an appendix to his (1901) edition of the Works, vol. iii. A draft of the second part of the *Principles* (§§ 85–145) is extant in another of Berkeley's notebooks[2]; it contains some interesting variants, which are noted in Jessop's edition of the *Principles*.

The *Principles* was published in Dublin in 1710 in the month of May. It is designated " Part I " on the title-

---

[1] MS. D. 5. 17 in the Library, T.C.D.

[2] British Museum, Add. MS. 39304, pp. 35–105; for further details, see Jessop and Luce, *Bibliography of George Berkeley*, p. 82.

page, and as we know from the *Commentaries* (508n), two more parts had been originally planned, Part II to deal with ethics and psychology, and Part III with natural philosophy. Part II was begun and considerable progress made, but the manuscript was lost during Berkeley's travels in Italy. The Berkeley-Percival correspondence [1] should be consulted for a picture of the reception of the work in London, and for some important statements by Berkeley about the general aim of the work and its relation to the *Essay on Vision*.

A second edition of the *Principles* was published in London in 1734, with a new edition of the *Three Dialogues* appended. There is at present no scholarly modern edition of the text of the second edition, and therefore I have taken my quotations [2] from the first edition, as edited by Professor T. E. Jessop (1937) with the second edition variants, etc.

Two more works belong to this period, *Passive Obedience* (1712) and *Three Dialogues Between Hylas and Philonous* (1713). The former consists of three discourses in College Chapel brought together to form a small treatise on ethical principles with a political reference. The *Three Dialogues* is one of the most beautiful works on philosophy in the English tongue. Its aim is " to treat more clearly and fully of certain principles laid down in the first [3] and to place them in a new light " (Preface). It is a dramatization of the argument for immaterialism, with Hylas as the matterist and Philonous representing Berkeley. The discussions of sameness and of creation in the third dialogue are more or less new ; but there are no other

[1] Rand, *Berkeley and Percival*, pp. 72–96.

[2] I have modernized the spelling in cases where the old spelling might distract the reader's attention, *e.g.* I have printed " knowledge " for Berkeley's " knowlege."

[3] *Sc.* Part, *i.e.* the *Principles*.

additions of importance, and there is no change of doctrine whatever. The Preface refers to the earlier works as containing fuller expressions of his views ; the *Principles* is in no sense superseded by the *Three Dialogues*, but remains as the adequate and main exposition of Berkeley's immaterialism. Accordingly I have focused attention upon the *Principles* in the following pages, and have cut down to a minimum my references to the *Three Dialogues*. I do not intend thereby any slight to the later work, which has a charm of its own and is invaluable as a *supplementary* account of immaterialism.

Berkeley's main philosophical work for posterity was done when he had published his *Principles*, and the remainder of his story shall be told merely in outline. It is enough for the reader to know that he was no crank, no mystic, no solitary, and that he had other things to do in life besides philosophy. He always remained a philosopher ; but there was nothing of the professor of philosophy in him. He had no motive for " developing " his philosophy, or for gathering round him a school of adherents. He did indeed propagate his views in America, not without success ; and he wrote several works later in life which build on immaterialism and apply it ; but he made no further systematic attempt (after the *Three Dialogues*) to re-argue the case. He seems to have felt that his case was complete, as I believe it to be, that it could hardly be bettered, and that if it did not win acceptance the responsibility was not his. Even a bishop may be allowed some proper pride, and his silence about matter in his later life is the silence of dignity, not of acquiescence, much less of withdrawal. Six months before his death he republished his *De Motu*, which gives the application of immaterialism to the problem of motion, and there is no shadow of reason for doubting the truth of Reid's words, written while men were alive who had known Berkeley, " It is probable the Bishop made but few converts to his doctrine ; but it is certain he made some ; and that he himself continued, to the end of his life, firmly persuaded, not only of its truth, but of its great importance for the improvement of human knowledge, and especially for the defence of religion." [1]

In treating his life four periods may conveniently be distinguished, the years of early authorship, already described, his travels in England and on the Continent, his American mission, and the Cloyne episcopate. [2]

In January 1713 Berkeley left Ireland for the first time and made his way to London. He went for reasons of health, to benefit by travel, and to meet "men of merit" ; he denies that he went to engage himself " in the interests of those in power " or to secure his own advancement. [3] He already had a reputation as a man of letters, and he had the *entrée* into the literary world, and soon became friends with Addison, Pope, and Steele. For Steele he wrote a number of essays in the *Guardian*. Swift befriended him, presented him at Court, introduced him to Lord Berkeley of Stratton (probably a distant kinsman) and other influential men in Church and State. That summer he spent two months at Oxford, and in the autumn he was appointed chaplain to the Earl of Peterborough

[1] *Intellectual Powers*, Essay II, chap. x.

[2] For details the following should be consulted, Stock's *Life*, 1776, and in the 1784 edition of the Works ; A. C. Fraser, *Life and Letters*, the standard biography, vol. iv in the 1871 edition ; B. Rand, *Berkeley and Percival* (1914), and *Berkeley's American Sojourn* (1932). Considering the extent of ground he covered, Fraser's *Life* is remarkably accurate ; but it needs to be checked with the letters and supplemented by reference to subsequent publications.

[3] The first two reasons are mentioned in the Queen's Letter, dated 9th of September 1713, granting leave of absence, which with four others (9th September 1715 ; 17th August 1717 ; 6th May 1719 ; 6th May 1721) is preserved in the Library, T.C.D. For his own statement about his reasons, see Rand, *Berkeley and Percival*, p. 124.

on the occasion of the latter's diplomatic mission to
Sicily. Berkeley spent a month in Paris, where arrange-
ments were made for a meeting with Malebranche ;
crossing the Alps he visited Turin, Genoa, Leghorn,
Florence, and other Italian cities. The death of the
queen terminated the mission, and Berkeley was back
in London in August 1714. In the following summer
he travelled in the west of England, and in the autumn
of 1716 his second and longer continental tour began.
This time he went as tutor to George Ashe, son of the
Bishop of Clogher, who was travelling for his health.
Again he crossed the Alps, and with his pupil spent
nearly four years in Italy and Sicily, visiting Rome
and most of the other famous cities. His travel diaries
covering part of the period are extant, and his eye-
witness account of an eruption of Vesuvius was com-
municated to the Royal Society. He returned to London
in the late summer or autumn of 1720, writing his *De
Motu* at Lyons on the way back. In September of the
following year he resumed his work in Trinity College.

The South Sea Bubble, a general pessimism [1] about
the social and moral state of the old world and " the
breath of hope " from the new, had turned men's eyes
westward.[2] Soon after he returned to Ireland Berkeley
conceived the plan of bringing Christian civilization to
America by establishing a college in Bermuda. There
young Indians and the sons of settlers were to be educated,

[1] See Berkeley's *An Essay Towards Preventing the Ruine of Great Britain*
(1721).

[2] Westward the course of Empire takes its way :
  The four first Acts already past,
  A fifth shall close the drama with the day :
  Time's noblest offspring is the last.

From Berkeley's " Verses on the Prospect of Planting Arts and Learning in
America," written in 1726, published in the *Miscellany* (1752).

and thence they were to return to the mainland imbued with Christian and cultural ideals. Berkeley embodied the scheme in his *A Proposal for the Better Supplying* . . . (1724). A legacy from Esther Vanhomrigh (Vanessa) and his appointment to the Deanery of Derry (1724) had made him financially independent, and he spent the next few years in commending his *Proposal* to the public and in seeking the support of influential public men. About £5,000 was received in subscriptions. The scheme was submitted to the law officers of the Crown, and was approved by them.[1] The king granted a charter to the college to be built in Bermuda. Parliament passed a resolution asking that provision for it should be made. The Treasury agreed to make a grant of £20,000 ; but the grant was to be a charge on the sale of public lands in St. Christopher's, and, it would seem, no date for the payment of the grant was fixed. Circumstances, amongst them the natural expectations of the subscribers, forced Berkeley to sail before the public money was available. Moreover, he now realized that Rhode Island would be a far better site for the college than Bermuda, and he may have hoped that by settling in Rhode Island and acquiring land there, he might be able to induce the Government to sanction the change.

In the summer of 1728 he married Anne, daughter of John Forster, who had been Speaker of the Irish House of Commons and, later, Lord Chief Justice. Shortly afterwards he and his bride and some friends set sail for America. He spent nearly three years in Newport, Rhode Island, where his house, Whitehall, is still an object of public interest, and is cared for in his memory by the Society of Colonial Dames on behalf of Yale Uni-

---

[1] For their Report, found by Dr. Chart and published by me, see *Hermathena*, vol. xxiii, 1933, p. 32.

versity, to whom Berkeley presented it. There in the shade of " the Hanging Rocks," fronting the Atlantic, he wrote *Alciphron : or the Minute Philosopher* (published 1732), a fine work in dialogue in detailed defence of Christian faith and order ; immaterialism is assumed (see dialogues iv and vii), but not obtruded. Hearing semi-officially that there was no prospect of the public money being paid, Berkeley was forced to abandon the enterprise, and he sailed from Boston, reaching England on the 30th of October 1731.

The great project had miscarried (" under a circumstance I could neither obviate nor foresee," *Alciphron*, I, i); its primary aim was not achieved, St. Paul's College in Bermuda was not built. But on the long view Berkeley's efforts were not in vain. Yale and Harvard benefited directly by his visit ; Columbia University and the University of Pennsylvania had the advantage of his counsel in their early days. The University of Berkeley, California, and the Berkeley Divinity School, New Haven, commemorate his name. " The inspiration and influence of Berkeley's visit and efforts have been of enduring value in the life and thought of America. Better possibly than the founding of a single college has been the intellectual stimulus felt on this continent, at first from his personal aid and counsel during his sojourn here, then more widely from his devotion to the cause of its higher education, and in all subsequent years more especially by the abiding impetus and supremacy of his idealistic philosophy." [1]

That Berkeley was not to blame for the outward failure of his mission was publicly recognized when the Crown appointed him to the bishopric of Cloyne in 1734. Of his nineteen years' episcopate little need be said here. He discharged the duties of his office diligently and

[1] B. Rand, *Berkeley's American Sojourn*, p. 67.

efficiently. He lived at Cloyne and rarely left his diocese. He superintended the education of his children, relieved distress, and cared for his flock. He used his powerful pen in several public questions. His *Analyst* (1734), with its two sequels in the following year, continued those " hints to the public " about infinitesimals which he had given twenty-five years previously in his *Principles* (§§ 123–134), and gave rise to a celebrated, long-continued, and fruitful controversy among mathematicians. His *Querist* (1735–37) was a landmark in the history of economics ; its principles were in advance of his day, and were in opposition to the prevailing mercantilist theory.

The best-known work of his later years is his *Siris*, first published in 1744 under the title *Philosophical reflexions and inquiries concerning the virtues of tar-water, and divers other subjects connected together and arising one from another.* The first portion of the work is devoted to the advocacy of tar-water as a medicine ; it had a wide, if transient, success ; many cures were reported, and tar-water was admitted to a place in the British pharmacopoeia, which it still holds. The second portion ranges unsystematically over a wide area of speculative philosophy and theology, and contains brilliant *aperçus* and great sayings. It neither announces nor contains a new philosophy or any departure from his old philosophy. The defence of Trinitarianism and the encouragement of the study of Greek philosophy are among its incidental aims ; its main aim, if it has one, is to exhibit God as the one true cause of change in the external world, and to trace His immediate operation through the whole chain of being (*Siris* § 237). But it is an unsystematic work with no definite plan or purpose beyond that of uplift in general. Berkeley himself calls it a " rude Essay," and it ought not to be spoken of in the same breath with the masterpieces of his youth. The modern notion that it was meant to supersede those masterpieces, or that it does in fact supersede them, is grotesquely untrue. Without any professed and open discussion of immaterialism,[1] the *Siris* chats about things in general from the standpoint of immaterialism. *An Immaterialist Looks At Life* would be the modern title for it. Its refutation of the mechanical philosophy and of Newton's theory of attraction are attacks on the very citadel of contemporary matterism (*ib*. §§ 220–50). The object of sense is no longer described in it as an " idea " ; " appearance " is substituted ; but that is only a change in technique, not in doctrine. Thirty-five years had elapsed since the *Principles* was written, and the term *idea* no longer served his turn, and Berkeley wisely dropped it ; but he did not drop the doctrine it had expressed. His theory of perception is unchanged ; for these " appearances " are " such as we see and perceive them ; their real and objective natures are, therefore, the same" (*Siris* § 292). They still form a rational discourse or language (*ib*. § 254), and they are still passive and without any power of agency or of cause (*ib*. § 155 *et passim*). Pure space, real spaces, corporeal forces, and absolute motions are still " phantoms " (*ib*. § 293).

Some commentators have represented Berkeley's immaterialism as a youthful indiscretion which he lived to repent and withdrew later in life. They are quite wrong, and are doing Berkeley a grave injustice. He was a convinced immaterialist in youth, in middle life, and in old age; and there is no hint at any retractation or withdrawal in his books or correspondence. In the writings of his contemporaries and immediate successors, so far as my reading has gone, there is no suggestion or suspicion that any such retractation or withdrawal occurred. In his

---

[1] *Siris* § 319 is the nearest approach to a direct argument about matter.

lifetime Berkeley was recognized as a leader of thought and a man of letters with a European reputation. Had he changed his mind on such a clear-cut issue, the change could never have passed unnoticed, and he was far too straightforward a man to wish to make the change surreptitiously.

To the evidence of Thomas Reid, quoted above (p. 12), let me add that of an even higher authority, the Bishop's wife. Mrs. Anne Berkeley was a well-educated, able woman with a fluent pen and a keen interest in religion and culture. Her son, writing in 1780 to W. S. Johnson, says that her powers of mind were as great as ever, and Johnson had described her when she was about seventy years old as " the finest old lady I ever saw, sensible, lively, facetious, and benevolent." [1] Her competence to speak about her husband's philosophy cannot be doubted. Now Stock's *Life* of Berkeley, published separately in 1776 with a second edition in 1777, was reprinted in the second volume of *Biographia Britannica* (1780, 2nd ed.), and the third volume (1784) contains a long series of remarks on that *Life* by the widow. Stock had said that Berkeley's disbelief in matter had sprung from, *inter alia*, " the airy visions of romances, to the reading of which he was addicted." Mrs. Berkeley takes him up sharply. She flatly denies that Berkeley was much addicted to reading romances, and she proceeds to give an intelligent account of one aspect of his immaterialism which amounts to a defence of it.[2] If he had abandoned immaterialism in middle life or old age, she

---

[1] *Yale University Library Gazette*, July 1933, pp. 30, 33.

[2] She says he " pursued Mr Locke's own mode of reasoning, and by it has demonstrated that the primary qualities of matter being as mutable as the secondary qualities, *both* alike deserve to be rejected. And if matter be possessed neither of primary nor of secondary qualities, the Bishop asks, ' Of what does it consist ? ' He pushes Mr Locke's argument home, and no further than truth and experiment lead." *Biog. Brit.*, vol. iii, 1784, Corrigenda and Addenda to vol. ii.

must have known about it, and she could not possibly have written, as she does, in vindication of his theory of matter, twenty or thirty years after his death. There is not a grain of truth, then, in the modern critic's damaging gibe to the effect that " Bishop Berkeley ceased to be a Berkeleian."

There is little more to record. In the summer of 1752 his son George was entered as a student at Christ Church, Oxford, and Berkeley with his wife and daughter went with him to see him settled in and to carry out, perhaps, what he had once called " my Oxford scheme." [1] He stood the journey well, and from Oxford he wrote a cheerful letter to the Bishop of Cork who was doing episcopal duties for him in Cloyne diocese ; but for some time he had been in failing health, and he died on Sunday the 14th of January 1753 at his residence in Holywell Street. He was buried in the chapel of Christ Church, where a memorial tablet is placed.

The views on Berkeley's teaching expressed by me in the following pages have been formed in the course of writing a number of monographs on specific problems of Berkeleian exegesis. The monographs are, of course, more heavily documented and more detailed than the book, and in case readers may wish to refer to them I append the list.

DOCTRINAL ARTICLES IN *Mind*
The Unity of the Berkeleian Philosophy, vol. xlvi, N.S., Nos. 181–82.
Development Within Berkeley's *Commonplace Book*, vol. xlix, N.S., No. 193

---

[1] Letter to Prior, 12th September 1746. Stock's *Life* says " He had taken a fixed resolution to spend the remainder of his days in this city [Oxford], with a view of indulging the passion for a learned retirement. . . ." Fraser bases on this passage a highly coloured picture of his intentions, which may or may not be founded on fact. It is clear that Berkeley had no intention of resigning his bishopric.

Berkeley's Existence in the Mind, vol. l, N.S., No. 199
The Alleged Development of Berkeley's Philosophy, vol. lii, N.S., No. 206

DOCTRINAL ARTICLES IN *Hermathena*

The Berkeleian Idea of Sense, No. lv, 1940
The Philosophical Correspondence Between Berkeley and Johnson, No. lvi, 1940
Mind-Dependence in Berkeley, No. lvii, 1941
Berkeley's Doctrine of the Perceivable, No. lx, 1942

OTHER ARTICLES

Berkeley's *Description of the Cave of Dunmore*, *Hermathena*, vol. xxi, 1931
Berkeley's *Commonplace Book*—Its Date, Purpose, Structure, and Marginal Signs, *Hermathena*, vol. xxii, 1932
Two Sermons by Bishop Berkeley, *Hermathena*, vol. xxii, 1932
Some Unpublished Berkeley Letters with Some New Berkeleiana, *Proc. R. I. Acad.*, vol. xli, C. 4, 1933
More Unpublished Berkeley Letters and New Berkeleiana, *Hermathena*, vol. xxiii, 1933
Berkeley's Bermuda Project and His Benefactions to American Universities, With Unpublished Letters and Extracts from the Egmont Papers, *Proc. R. I. Acad.*, vol. xlii, C. 6, 1934
Two Sermons by Bishop Berkeley, *Proc. R. I. Acad.*, vol. xliii, C. 8, 1936
The Purpose and the Date of Berkeley's *Commonplace Book*, *Proc. R. I. Acad.*, vol. xlviii, C. 7, 1943
Berkeley's Essays in the *Guardian*, *Mind*, vol. lii, N.S., No. 207
Immaterialism, *Proc. Brit. Acad.*, vol. xxx.

ERPRETATIONS

not " Christian Science " ;
Berkeley died at Oxford on
d was buried *six* days later
Church.   This long interval
vas no accident ; it was pre-
1s of his will, dated the 31st
ment commends his soul to
xtremely frank directions for
er death.[1]   It is not surprising
s separated soul ; but many
tructions about his dead body.
;ed with denying the existence
dies and of his own body, and
ince as generated by the act
1 solemn document he testifies
imo belief in their existence, when his senses
longer function, his brain will think no more,
his spirit will have gone away.   He took his early
philosophy seriously ; he remained true to it to the end
of his life,[2] and those who would master it must forget
the foolish Berkeley of gossip and tradition, and must
fix their gaze on the sane and sensible author of the

[1] " Item, that my Body, before it is buried, be kept five days above
ground or longer, even till it grow offensive by the cadaverous smell, and
that during the said time it lye unwashed, undisturbed, and covered by
the same bed clothes in the same bed, the head being raised upon the
pillows."   Fraser, *Life and Letters*, p. 345.   (See article on " Precipitant
Burials " in the *Dublin Journal*, 4th August 1747.)

[2] See my " The Alleged Development of Berkeley's Philosophy,"
Mind, vol. lii, N.S., No. 206.

Principles, who all his life believed in soul and body, whose thought and action mirrored that belief.[1]

His immaterialism is *not* acosmism ; his denial of matter is not a denial of the world. Some romantics can wish the world away, and, for them, it is gone. Berkeley's thought is not romantic, much less narcotic ; there is no defeatism in his attitude, no " escapism " in his method ; there could be no " flight from the world " for him. On the contrary, he comes forth like a giant to grasp the world and set it at arm's length, that he may study it and understand it and absorb its meaning. He looked at it steadily, and saw that it is a world of sense and not a world of matter. His immaterialism is not an old man's dream, but a young man's vision. He denied the fancy in order to affirm and confirm the fact. He so denied matter as to affirm the sensible.

His immaterialism is *not* pantheism. Berkeley was a theist, loyal to his creed, and pantheism was not in him. He believed in the world of sense, which is other than God ; he believed in the society of finite spirits, which is other than God. He could not hold or teach that all is God, or that God is all. He saw all things in God ; he saw the human mind and human knowledge as in God ; he saw the world of sense as the work of God ; he saw, as does orthodox Christianity, God every-where and working all, in all ; he was a panentheist, but no pantheist.

Berkeley's immaterialism is not *panpsychism*. Of all the mistaken interpretations commonly placed on

[1] " I see no difficulty in conceiving a change of state, such as is vulgarly called death, as well without as with material substance. It is sufficient for that purpose that we allow sensible bodies, *i.e.* such as are immediately perceived by sight and touch ; the existence of which I am so far from questioning (as philosophers are used to do), that I establish it, I think, upon evident principles." Berkeley to Johnson, 25th November 1729.

Berkeley's teaching the panpsychist is the most plausible, the most excusable (in hasty readers), and the furthest from the truth. Panpsychism is the humanist's equivalent for pantheism. The pantheist teaches that all is God, the panpsychist teaches that all is mind. Now a philosopher, reared, as Berkeley was, on the Cartesian doctrine of mind and matter, on first contact with immaterialism, is predisposed for panpsychism. If mind and matter be the sum total of reality, and you take away matter, the remainder is mind. I can believe that Berkeley performed that subtraction sum at first ; I do not assert that he did so, for I am not sure. On the second page of a private notebook [1] which he filled some three years before the publication of the *Principles*, he wrote :

> Nothing properly but persons *i.e.* conscious things do exist, all other things are not so much existences as manners of ye existence of persons.

That sentiment is panpsychist, or nearly so ; but there is nothing like it in his published works, and much that is irreconcilable with it. He may have been just toying with the notion ; he may have been deliberately trying it out. But if he was ever in the morass he was not long in struggling out ; for shortly afterwards he wrote in the companion notebook :

> We have an intuitive knowlege of the existence of other things besides our selves & even praecedaneous to the knowlege of our own existence. . .[2]

No panpsychist could write those words. It is certain that months before he went to press Berkeley had fought clear of monistic immaterialism and the doctrine that all is mind, and had reached a dualistic immaterialism which

[1] *PC* 24, where see my note.   [2] *PC* 547.

accepts the reality both of mind and of body unperceived by man.   That is the immaterialism of the *Principles*, expounded in the following pages.

Berkeley's immaterialism is not panpsychism, nor pantheism, nor acosmism, nor is it a rejection of sensible body.   From my four denials the young student will gather that grave misinterpretations of Berkeley's teaching are current, and he will, I hope, infer that the chief initial difficulty in the path of Berkeleian studies is that of understanding the true issue and of seeing clearly what Berkeley is driving at.[1]   The root of the trouble is that the term *matter* is ambiguous, and is popularly, though unphilosophically, used to describe sensible things or sensible bodies in their more general aspects.   I, therefore, venture to beg the novice who wishes to master the authentic teaching of the historic Berkeley, to keep on reminding himself that the *matter* at issue, *i.e.* the material substance which Berkeley denied (*a*) is not sensible body or sensible parts of body, is not an actual or possible object of sense, is nothing that we see or touch (or hear or taste or smell), but (*b*) is a " something we know not what," a guess-substance, a conjecture of the ancient Greeks, a something vaguely supposed to serve as invisible, intangible, non-spiritual support of all that we actually see and touch.

Man perceives a world.   Berkeley's philosophy is a serious and sustained attempt to understand through an analysis of perception itself those features of the perceived world which interest man as a moral being.   It deserves a patient hearing, at least.   I have, I trust, made out a *prima facie* case for it.   I have shown that it is not flagrantly opposed to commonsense.   It is a striking theory,

---

[1] Berkeley himself says so : " but, above all things, you should beware of imposing on yourself by that vulgar sophism which is called *ignoratio elenchi*. . . ."   *Three Dialogues*, iii, *ad fin.*

but not a shocking theory. Surely it has a strong claim to be heard anew, correctly interpreted and documented, in these days in which materialism,[1] not content with threatening religion, is invading politics, ethics, history, sociology, and art, and is therefore threatening our received way of life and thought.

I could close this chapter here ; but I must make one more denial. I risk involving myself in a barren controversy about a label ; but labels are important to travellers, including travellers in the realm of mind. I am asking students of Berkeley to go " back to Berkeley." I am putting forward a new-old view of his philosophy, and therefore I take my courage in my two hands, and deny that Berkeley was an idealist.

Newspapers mean by *idealist* a man who believes in God, the soul, and duty—a man who has ideals and tries to live up to them. In that wide sense, of course, Berkeley was an idealist. I use the term as it is used in philosophy to-day. I mean by idealism that type of philosophical doctrine found in the recognized idealists— Kant, Hegel, and Bradley. If those three are idealists, then Berkeley is not, and his teaching can be assimilated to theirs only by being misrepresented. To come to Berkeley after reading Kant, or Hegel, or Bradley is like coming from a hothouse into the open air.

Berkeley nowhere calls himself an idealist.[2] He once

[1] *Materialism* has come to mean the doctrine that *all* is matter. I use the term *matterism* for the doctrine that matter exists ; hence I describe as " matterists " (without giving offence, I trust) all thinkers who believe in the existence of matter, whatever their views on mind and spirit ; in this terminology, of course, there are many " matterists " who are not " materialists."

[2] Norris published his *Theory of the Ideal World*, 1701–4. I presume he was the English idealist of the day ; but no one would class him with Berkeley. The term *ideist* was known in Berkeley's day, and was applied by John Sargent to Locke, not without reason ; for Locke resolves all objects of knowledge, as such, into ideas.

speaks of "ideal knowledge"[1] meaning thereby knowledge of ideas as distinct from knowledge of spirits. A materialist is, strictly, one who believes that all is matter, and by analogy an idealist should be one who believes that all is idea. Berkeley believes nothing of the sort.

Who first called Berkeley an idealist I cannot say. Sir William Hamilton, who uses the label, may have been following Kant. I suspect that the prevalence of the practice is due to Kant, who in his *Refutation of Idealism* takes Berkeley as typical of dogmatical idealism. If Satan may rebuke sin, Kant may refute idealism ; but he has no right to say, as he does, in that *Refutation*[2] that Berkeley "maintains that space, together with all the objects of which it is the inseparable condition, is a thing which is in itself impossible, and that consequently the objects in space are mere products of the imagination." Those words are not even a burlesque of Berkeley's teaching ; they bear no relation whatever to it. Kant must have been speaking from hearsay ; and if he is responsible for labelling Berkeley an idealist, it is clear that the label is, by origin, a libel, and was affixed in ignorance of the facts.

To-day they even call him " the father of modern idealism." What a remarkable accident of birth this is ! Berkeley is the putative father of modern idealism, and the child does not take after its father in the slightest degree. No historical affiliation can be traced, no doctrinal debt established, and the cliché, if it has any objective reference, ought to stand for some deep affinity of spirit. But who can seriously consider Berkeley as the spiritual father of Kant or Hegel or Bradley ? They would turn in their graves, all four, at the very thought. What has the author of *Alciphron* in common with one

[1] *Princ.* § 97.   [2] Tr. Meiklejohn, p. 166.

who saw our orthodox theology vanish like a ghost " before the daylight of free sceptical inquiry " and felt it as " the mutilation of our nature " ? [1]

If we make idealism consist in a denial of an external world independent of experience, we are narrowing unduly the usual suggestion of the term, and adopting an ambiguous criterion ; but even so the term hardly applies to Berkeley. He denied an external world which no experience can reach ; he denied an external world in the outer darkness, unseen, unknown, uncared for ; but a world existing prior to your mind and mine he affirms, and he more than once affirms its externality and independence, and because he believed in that external, independent world, he made testamentary dispositions about his body.

The term *idealism* to-day connotes a distrust of the senses and an exaggerated estimate of the powers of the human mind ; in both those respects Berkeley is non-idealist. Idealists usually depreciate sentience, oppose their reason to their senses, and regard the sensible world as an illusion or a problem. Berkeley gives sentience its due place in the cognitive system ; he trusts the evidence of sense, and accepts the world of sense, declaring its reality, and giving it an assured place in his metaphysic. Idealists claim much, often too much, for the human mind ; often they fail to distinguish it from the divine mind ; they regard man's mind as determinant of knowledge, constitutive of reality, imposing its forms and categories, like creative spirit moving on the formless deep. There is nothing of all that in Berkeley. Idealists have fastened on Berkeley's New Principle, *esse est percipi*, and have made it mean what Berkeley never intended it to mean ; they have been attracted by the spirituality of his system, and

[1] Bradley, *Appearance and Reality*, Introd.

have sought aid from it.   But in his conceptions of God, of the finite spirit, of the senses, of the external world, of cause, of the imagination, and of the general nature of knowing, Berkeley is so remote from the typical idealist positions that it is sheer nonsense to call him an idealist. I should add that I am speaking of the author of the *Principles*, not of the Berkeley of the stage and the text-book, not of " the good bishop " so easily " vanquished with a grin." [1]

Kuno Fischer said that Berkeley was " no idealist, but a complete realist." [2]   A. C. Fraser, too, called him a realist.   I am not concerned to do so.   Non-idealists are not necessarily realists ;   it may be that both terms are here out of place.   Anyhow, the term *realist* is nearly as ambiguous as *idealist*.   The old realists would have been scandalized by Berkeley's empiricism, and would have rejected his account of universals.   Some modern realists would reject his doctrine of spirit.   This much, however, can be said with confidence.   In his general attitude to the problem of knowing he is far closer to modern realism than to modern idealism.   Knowing, for Berkeley, is a finding, and not a making.   He looked straight at things, and faced up to them, as realists try to do.   He sets his object at arm's length.   He looks out of the open window, and not into the mirror.   He believed in direct awareness ; he sees directly and without any cognitive medium the world in which he lives and acts.   He rejects repre-sentationism and the three-term theory of knowing and perceiving, and he is always loyal to the subject-object relation.

Mystic, nominalist, solipsist, sceptic, sensationalist, Platonist, all these epithets have been hurled at Berkeley

---

[1] " And coxcombs vanquish Berkeley with a grin "—Brown.
[2] Quoted by W. Graham, *Idealism* (1872), p. 113.

in praise or blame. In my opinion none of them applies, but as descriptions they are all too partial to come within the scope of this introductory chapter, and the better way of dealing with them is to set before the reader the true interpretation, as I see it, of what Berkeley actually wrote—which I now proceed to do.

CHAPTER II

CONCRETE THINKING

(Berkeley's Introduction to the *Principles*)

" I HAVE always thought and judged for myself," [1] so wrote Berkeley in later life. He studied Locke and Malebranche, and he learned much from them and from many others ; but he would not follow any thinker blindly, or one inch beyond the truth as he saw it. If readers are to enter into the spirit of his immaterialism, they must capture that spirit of free inquiry from which it sprang. Berkeley made his discovery because his was a liberty-loving mind in the golden age of philosophical liberty. He lived and thought in a free country, in that all-too-brief period between the old order and the new, when a man had no need to concern himself overmuch with what Aristotle and other great men taught, when no philosopher dared attempt to write a final philosophy, or put truth in a strait-jacket. In his day any man of education in a free community felt free to seek for himself the truth of things, without attaching himself to a " school," or ploughing through half a dozen systems of dead philosophy. In that free, pioneering spirit [2] Berkeley fixed his gaze on a table or a tree, and asked himself the question, Is there a material table or tree over and above the table or tree I see and touch ? It is a question of fact, not of academic philosophy. Berkeley considered that any free and fearless thinker ought to be able to decide for himself what the factors in perception really

---

[1] *Defence of Free-thinking*, § 19.   [2] *Cf. PC* 266, 279, 556.

are, and therefore ought to be able to make up his mind, without help from authority, as to whether there are reasonable grounds for supposing the existence of material substance. He writes as a freeman for free men, and only in that spirit of utter intellectual freedom can his book be profitably read.

A feeling for reality and the concrete, involving a rejection of the hoary abstractions of the schools, was a second characteristic of Berkeley's thought, not unconnected with his love of liberty. He is resolved to dig down to the facts of the perceptual situation, and see for himself who's who and what's what. He is resolved to get rid of the fog of time-honoured phrases and verbal substitutes for reality, and see clearly what actually happens when a man perceives. That is why his speculations, two hundred and thirty years old, are fresh and living to-day. He formed the habit of concrete thinking. To induce the same habit in his readers is the aim of his Introduction ; he tries to prepare " the mind of the reader for the easier conceiving what follows," and to refute " the opinion that the mind hath a power of framing abstract ideas or notions of things." (§ 6.)

Not a word is said about matter in the Introduction. Berkeley purposely omitted all mention of it.[1] In consequence some critics have failed to see the relevance of the attack on abstract ideas, and have even said that Berkeley makes no use of the results of his Introduction in the body of the work. That is a short-sighted view.[2]

---

[1] " Whatever doctrine contradicts vulgar and settled opinion had need been introduced with great caution into the world. For this reason it was I omitted all mention of the non-existence of matter in the title-page, dedication, preface, and introduction, that so the notion might steal unawares on the reader. . . ." Rand, *Berkeley and Percival*, p. 82.

[2] I have answered it below, p. 36. Hume (*Treatise*, I, vii) calls Berkeley's attack on abstract ideas " one of the greatest and most valuable discoveries that has been made of late years in the republic of letters."

The Introduction has an important function ; it puts the reader into the right attitude of mind, and makes him think in terms of the concrete, showing him that material substance is an abstract idea, and explaining why abstractionists are inveterately disposed to think that matter exists.

The details of the argument need not detain us long. Berkeley's method is simple. He selects Locke as the typical exponent of abstraction, and says to the reader, This is the abstract idea, which Locke says we must frame if we are to have general knowledge. I have tried to frame an abstract idea after the Lockian pattern, and I cannot do so. Can you ?

Abstract idea was an accepted abbreviation for *abstract general idea*, and meant a general idea framed by a process of abstraction from particulars, such as the abstract idea of motion framed by abstracting the common element in particular movements. Locke states his doctrine "*ex professo*" in Book II xi 9 and Book III iii 6. In the second of these passages he says, " Ideas become general by separating from them the circumstances of time and place and any other ideas that may determine them to this or that particular existence. By this way of abstraction they are made capable of representing more individuals than one ; each of which, having in it a conformity to that abstract idea, is (as we call it) of that sort." The abstract idea is thus what is in our mind corresponding to the essence or species *in rerum natura*. Now when Locke consciously formulated the view that our knowledge does not extend beyond our ideas, the abstract idea came gradually into the forefront of the picture, and in Book IV it dominates the scene ; " It is the contemplation of our own abstract ideas that alone is able to afford us general knowledge " (IV vi 16). In the following chapter

Locke gives his famous description of the abstract idea of a triangle. " It must be neither oblique, nor rectangle, neither equilateral, equicrural, nor scalenon ; but all and none of these at once."

For Berkeley this passage was a *reductio ad absurdum* of the doctrine of abstraction, and his attack on it he calls " the killing blow " [1] This idea which we are supposed to frame, this acme and goal of general knowledge, is a thing impossible. Try it for yourself, he says. Try to frame this abstract idea of a triangle with all these contradictory attributes and none of them. It cannot be done. That is his refutation of abstract ideas.

The basis of the refutation seems somewhat narrow, especially considering all that has been built upon it by friend and foe. Berkeley has clearly scored against Locke and has made a great breach in the Lockian epistemology. Has he done more ? Does his refutation of abstract ideas refute any error to-day ? His Introduction has abiding value as a buttress of immaterialism, but does it pronounce on the nature of knowledge ? Does it solve, does it set out to solve, our epistemological problems ? These questions are not easy to answer, for the Introduction suffers somewhat from divided aims which come to light when the reader goes behind the attack on Locke and tries to pin-point the *positive* teaching. Berkeley is mainly concerned with the limits of abstraction, but he is also dealing with the origin and nature of universals. A further complication is the fact that he is here arguing to some extent on the principles of others ; he is no representationist, but in refuting Locke he uses *ad hominem* the language of representationism.

[1] *PC* 687.

Berkeley himself considered that he had done more than prove Locke wrong. He regarded his Introduction as a positive contribution to epistemological truth ; he held that it exposed a false principle of knowledge with wide ramifications. Whether or not these claims can be sustained need not be determined here. Our business is with immaterialism, and from that standpoint the Introduction serves its purpose well.[1] It ought neither to be undervalued nor overworked. Possibly its account of general and particular is not adequate ; perhaps its epistemology is not consistent in every detail ; none the less it does what an introduction should do ; it introduces the main theme in a persuasive manner ; it creates the right atmosphere ; it prepares the way for immaterialism by turning our attention from abstractions and disposing us to think in terms of the concrete.

We must carefully note that Berkeley does not deny abstraction *in toto*. As the faculty of analysis he accepts it. But no analysis could yield Locke's abstract idea of a triangle ; it is not the result of taking to pieces what is there, but, if I may so say, of putting together what is not there. And, as a lover of truth, Berkeley had to say, This is mere obscurantism. Analysis, the power of considering separately separable parts, is an undeniable psychological fact ; and if that is all that is meant by abstraction, Berkeley would not dream of denying it. He denied such abstractions as motion apart from moving things, existence apart from existent things, and matter apart from things of sense. He states his position as follows :

---

[1] Place Collier's *Clavis Universalis* (1713) side by side with the *Principles*, and you appreciate the value of Berkeley's Introduction. Both books teach immaterialism, but Collier's is a weak and spineless argument compared with Berkeley's, and part of the reason is that Berkeley's argument is pushed home by the attack on abstract ideas, and Collier's is not.

" To be plain, I own myself able to abstract in one sense, as when I consider some particular parts or qualities separated from others, with which thô they are united in some object, yet it is possible they may really exist without them. But I deny that I can abstract from one another, or conceive separately, those qualities which it is impossible should exist so separated ; or that I can frame a general notion by abstracting from particulars in the manner aforesaid." (§ 10)[1].

In the second part of the Introduction (§§ 18*ff.*), Berkeley traces the error to the abuse of language. It has been wrongly assumed, he says, that all significant words stand for ideas, and that the only function of language is the communication of ideas. But we do in fact use words without any cognitive content ; we use them to raise hopes, fears, etc., in our hearers. There are no ideas (in Locke's sense) corresponding to such words. Not grasping this fact, men when they found general names in use have jumped to the conclusion that there must be abstract general ideas corresponding to them. It follows, then, that if we wish to rid ourselves of the habit of abstract thinking and substitute the habit of concrete thinking, we must watch our words ; as far as possible we must consider our ideas in isolation from the words which commonly express them, and thus we shall "get clear of all controversies purely verbal." In particular we must watch haloed words like " material substance," which were part of the technique of ancient Greek philosophy, words which have survived when their meaning has long since passed away. For

[1] From this position Berkeley never varied. Attempts have been made to show that he modified his doctrine in the second edition, and gave it up towards the end of his life ; but these attempts cannot succeed. Berkeley never modified nor withdrew his original attack on abstract ideas ; see *PC* 318*n.*

such words obscure the concrete facts and confound our reasoning.[1]

Having shown the importance of the Introduction, I can now grant that it is not all-important, and that a student need not weary himself over its details if his main concern is with Berkeley's argument against matter. The refutation of matter does not *rest* on the refutation of abstract ideas ; but the one refutation greatly helps our appreciation and understanding of the other. It would be a mistake to regard the Introduction as an irrelevant piece of reasoning put there to match Locke's attack on innate ideas. The scores of entries in the *Commentaries* marked *I*, and the Draft Introduction, so carefully penned, are manuscript testimony to the high importance Berkeley himself attached to it. Time and again in the body of the work he clinches an argument with, " To say no more ; it is an *abstract idea*," or similar words. Matter and existence are the two chief abstractions in view, but the abstract ideas of extension, figure, motion, unity, presence, quiddity, entity, time, place, space, happiness, goodness, justice, virtue are all mentioned in the *Principles*, and they all fall beneath Berkeley's " Razor." The doctrine of abstract ideas is one of the two " secret, un-examined errors " (§ 118) diffused through all the branches of mathematics ; it has infected, he holds, ethics, physics, and other disciplines. Therefore whoever wishes to go beyond Berkeley's bare denial of matter, and will enter into the spirit of his constructive philosophy, must allow full weight to his rejection of abstract ideas.

Berkeley's call to concrete thinking is like the modern call to direct awareness. Like the realist of to-day, he

[1] In the Draft Introduction, as in his *Commentaries*, Berkeley stresses in this connection the conceit of the solitary, speechless philosopher (see *PC* 566n) ; and he himself seems to have conducted some experiments in voluntary silence or wordless thought (*PC* 600).

is against roundabout ways of knowing. He is determined to think what he thinks and not some substitute object. Contact your object, he says, your immediate object, and you will see through abstract ideas like matter and existence. Contact your object. Consider the actual colour you see and the actual roughness you touch, and you will not be led away off to the futile chase of abstractions, the will o' the wisp, the something round the corner, the something over the hill, the " something we know not what."

CHAPTER III

THE PERCEIVED OBJECT

(Principles, § 1)

THE first seven sections of the *Principles* contain the essence of Berkeley's case. In section 1 he analyses the perceived object, and in section 2 the perceiving subject. In section 3 he explains the " existence " of the percept. In sections 4 and 5 he gives the reason why people mis-read the perceptual situation. In section 6 he indicates the infinite factor in perception. In section 7 he surveys the whole field and draws the conclusion, " there is not any other substance than *spirit,* or that which perceives " —*i.e.* there is no material substance. Thus quietly, methodically, and without naming matter Berkeley builds up his argument and makes the notion of immaterialism " steal unawares on the reader." He shows us, as it were, an air graph of the perceptual situation ; here are its factors, the sensible object, the sentient subject, and God. If that be the full account, then there is no need for material substance, or room for it ; matter's occupation's gone.

He assumes—a correct assumption—that the problem of matter is a problem of perception. There are, indeed, other lines of argument ; we may reason *pro* and *con* about the supposed infinite divisibility of matter, about the conservation of matter, about matter as the basis of change ; but these are long-range secondary arguments. The philosopher's primary concern is with what is nearer home, the percept and the percipient. His task is to interpret what is actually presented to our senses here and now in the very gateway of knowledge ; for unless there is matter in the table I see before me and on which my elbow rests, there is no matter in the ground beneath it, or in the sky above.

In this chapter we consider section 1. The first sentence gives a " survey " of the objects of knowledge, and in it we have to examine briefly a clause whose meaning has been disputed. The rest of the section is a studied and carefully worded analysis of the object perceived ; we must examine it at length, for it leads to the heart of Berkeley's immaterialism.

Objects of knowledge, says Berkeley, fall into three classes ; they are (1) ideas of sense, (2) " such as are perceived by attending to the passions and operations of the mind," (3) ideas of memory and the imagination. There is no initial difficulty about the first and the third classes ; ideas of sense are examined in the rest of this section and throughout the book ; ideas of the imagination (which covers memory) are examined in sections 28–33, and are there distinguished from ideas of sense. But what are we to make of class 2 ? What objects fall under it ? It is clear to me that the objects we perceive " by attending to the passions and operations of the mind " are ourselves, other finite spirits, and God. These objects, together with ideas, make up the full tale of objects studied in the *Principles*, and Berkeley could not possibly omit any of them from his opening " survey." It is a roundabout way of saying, what is said clearly later, that there are two main types of knowable objects, and only two—spirits and ideas.

Disputes have arisen because commentators, following Fraser, have made the grammatical and exegetical mis-

take [1] of supplying " ideas " after " such," instead of
" objects." Ideas perceived by attending to the operations of the mind do not exist for Berkeley. They could
not be fitted into his system. One of his cardinal contentions, urged over and over again, is that there are no
ideas of the mind or its operations. To make him disrupt
his whole philosophy in his opening sentence is un-
pardonable. He had considered the wording of the
opening sentence [2] and the apparent vagueness is probably
not due to carelessness, but to design. The passage is
reminiscent of Locke, and Lockian readers would naturally
take these words to mean " ideas of reflection." Berkeley
was a diplomatic writer, and may well have been content
that they should so take the words *at first*. He no more
accepts Locke's ideas of reflection than he accepts his
ideas of sense ; but he would have found it awkward to
explain at the outset his technical reasons against ideas
of the mind and its operations.

The remainder of the section gives Berkeley's analysis
of the perceived object. The ease and simplicity of the
language mask the gravity of the issue ; if what Berkeley
says here is correct, then he has proved at least half of his
case against matter. He takes the special senses, one by
one, sight, touch, smell, taste, and hearing, and then,
directly or by implication, he describes the objects of the
senses, one and all, as ideas. That is his first great step.
The hurrying reader, fresh from Locke's *Essay*, may easily
go wrong here, saying to himself, " Of course we mustn't
take the words too literally ; Berkeley is giving the name
idea to the picture of the object of sense or to the mental
handle by which we take hold of it. He doesn't mean

[1] G. A. Johnston has argued the point well, *Development of Berkeley's Philosophy*, pp. 143*ff.*
[2] See *PC* 571.

that the very objects themselves are ideas." But Berkeley does mean that the very objects themselves are ideas. He goes on to identify the perceived object with the sensible thing *without remainder*, arguing that all so-called *things* are made up of such objects " observed to accompany each other," and therefore " marked by one name." Accordingly all things of sense, organic, inorganic, natural or artificial, tree, apple, stone, book, are in their lowest common denominator " collections of ideas."

" Collections of ideas "—here is the sting of the section ; this is the first challenge to the matterist ; and here many readers will, I doubt not, " come to a stand and will call to mind many things." [1] A book might be called a collection of ideas metaphorically, but said of the apple we eat, the tree we climb, or the stone we throw, it sounds queer. But its strangeness is lessened when we see that by the phrase Berkeley is telling us what he means by " idea " as well as what he means by " thing." He can call a sensible thing " a collection of ideas," just because his ideas of sense are the sort of objects which can compose things. His ideas of sense are sensible ideas. [2]

" Collections of ideas "—the words should be read, not in mockery, but with intelligent sympathy and in their historical perspective. They were written over two hundred and thirty years ago, and in the interval their colloquial meaning has not changed, but their philosophical suggestion has greatly changed. There lies the root of the trouble. The phrase occurs in Locke's *Essay* (II xxvi 1) [3] whence, no doubt, Berkeley borrowed it. He did not mean by it quite what Locke

[1] Spinoza, *Ethics*, II, xi.

[2] " I am not for changing things into ideas, but rather ideas into things." *Three Dialogues*, iii *ad med.*

[3] " The substance wood which is a certain collection of simple ideas." Berkeley takes note of the passage in *PC* 179 ; *cf.* 512.

meant; but the loan was useful, because Locke's *Essay* was amazingly influential, and the phrase would not have sounded bizarre to philosophers of that day. Thanks to Locke the term *idea* was then the recognized and normal description of the immediate object of sense, and Berkeley could not avoid it, any more than a philosopher writing on perception to-day can avoid using the term " sense datum " or " sensum " for that object. Fashions in philosophy change; what is a sense datum to-day was a sensation yesterday, and an idea the day before yesterday. Berkeley had to use the technique of his day; he had to put his new wine into old bottles; and when he said that sensible things are collections of ideas, he meant exactly what those philosophers mean to-day who say that sensible things are collections of sense data. When we are weighing the phrase, therefore, we must banish from our minds the common use of the term *idea*. I have an idea of the North Pole, I say; that is, I have a mental picture of an arctic waste, framed by the imagination, or worked up from the data of memory, a representation or copy of reality, but not reality itself. Berkeley has a niche for ideas of that sort, too; he calls them " ideas of the imagination," assigns them important functions, and discusses them in sections 30–33; but on no account will he allow them to be confused with ideas of sense. His ideas of sense and those of the imagination have something in common, of course, or he would not call them both *ideas*; both types are first things in knowing; both are right up against the mind; both are immediate objects; both are passive; but there the resemblance stops. In their nature, their origin, and their functioning they are poles apart. The ideas of sense are sensible ideas; the ideas of the imagination are not.

When, therefore, Berkeley calls sensible things, like

chairs and tables, " collections of ideas," he is far from meaning that they are made up of mental imagery, mind-stuff, memory images or mental copies of reality ; he means the very opposite ; he means that they are *sensible* realities in whole and part and particle ; he means that they are what we see and feel them to be—that, truly that, but no more than that. He could have called them *things* (see § 39) ; he often does so ; but when he is speaking precisely, he prefers for technical reasons, which were good reasons in his day, to call them *ideas*.

Here are his reasons : ideas, *e vi termini*, are immediate objects, passive objects, and significant objects ; they are what is right in front of us ; they are *given* ; they are inactive, and they are in necessary relation to mind. The Berkeleian idea of sense is characterized by immediacy, passivity, and significance or relatedness to mind. These are its moments, or distinctive features, to which Berkeley recurs over and over again. Every sensible thing, then, every object of sense is, on this showing, just what it professes to be ; it is what it appears to be ; it is its appearances ; it is just what we sense, or may sense ; it is the sum, or collection, of its actual and possible sights and sounds, and tastes, and smells, and touches.

This account of the perceived object is so simple and natural that the sophisticated call it "naïve." Readers should try it out for themselves in concrete cases, and they will find that loyalty to the simple does not make a man a simpleton. This " naïve " theory has far-reaching consequences. If a given log of wood is what we see and touch and otherwise sense, that, and only that, then its matter or material substance is an empty name, like phlogiston, a relic of an out-worn philosophy. I may saw through the log with a cross-cut ; I may burn it ; I may apply to it all the resources of chemistry and physics, but I shall never come on its matter; I shall never find in it anything but what is sensible. I may cut into a Christmas pudding and may chance to find a sixpence, but I shall not find matter; the presumption is that matter is not there to find. The pudding's inside, like its outside, consists of things seen and touched and smelled and tasted; its interior is continuous with and homogeneous with those brown, soft, tasty, fragrant objects which constitute its exterior; by such objects and such objects alone I know it for what it is; such are the objects which we call sense data (or sensa), and which Berkeley called ideas of sense; such are the objects which, collected together, constitute a sensible thing; and of sensible things, so constituted, the sensible world consists.

There are two remarks to be made on the term *collection*. First, it might suggest a random assemblage, a haphazard gathering without principle and order. It might suggest that, but it need not do so, and Berkeley does not intend it to do so. Like other folk, he is unable to say all at once all he has to say. Like a cunning artist he is content to wait and leave something in suspense, and, honest empiricist that he is, he is content to describe piecemeal what comes along, knowing that the perfected description is the full explanation. " Master the whole, before you censure the part " is the burden of Berkeley's Preface to the *Principles*, and they break this canon who charge him with particularism and " atomistic sensationalism." They think of his ideas of sense as particles or atoms floating in a void, or " ruining along the illimitable inane." But Berkeley's main aim in calling the objects of sense *ideas* is to bring them within the range and orbit of ordering mind. Ideas, he says, " are not any how and at random produced, there being a certain order and connection between them, like to that of cause and

effect." [1]   A certain colour on the apple argues a certain
taste.   Lightning means thunder near, and rosy-fingered
dawn points to the sunrise.   Collecting is the work of
mind, and therefore " a collection of ideas " is a proper
phrase to describe the Berkeleian thing of sense, which
is a system of ordered objects forming part of a system of
ordered things.

But the phrase has a further implication, not quite
so obvious as the first, and requiring to be thought out.
A collection of ideas implies the perceivable as well as the
perceived.   If a sensible thing is a collection of ideas, it
must, from the nature of the case, be a collection of ideas
perceivable and ideas perceived.   To any such " collection," say an apple or a table, several senses contribute ;
it is a " collection " of data from sight, touch, hearing,
taste, and smell ; and you or I cannot possibly apprehend
all those data or ideas all at one time.   A finite mind
must take them in successively.   While, for instance, I
am admiring the hue of the Blenheim orange on the tree,
I cannot be perceiving the taste and smell of its interior ;
but I might perceive them, if I reach out my hand and
pluck the apple, and take a fruit-knife and set to work.
While I am actually perceiving certain of its visible ideas
(to return to Berkeley's technique), I cannot be perceiving
certain of its olfactory and " gustatory " ideas.   There is
depth in every " collection of ideas " as well as surface,
and to any observer of such a " collection " at a given
time, the ideas must fall into two classes, ideas perceived
and ideas waiting to be perceived.   Of the ideas-in-waiting
(if the phrase may pass) Berkeley says little, but he says
enough.   Naturally he wants to put the spotlight on the
perceived, and that, no doubt, is why in the first sentence
of the work he specifies " ideas actually imprinted on the

[1] § 64, *cf.* § 30.

senses." But those-to-be-perceived are never far from his thoughts. The problem of the perceivable is one of the most carefully studied problems in the *Commentaries*,[1] and Berkeley has his eye on it, even when he appears to ignore it. Critics have misunderstood his silences, because, I presume, they have not read all his utterances. They have often said that his system has no room for the perceivable ; they have represented his ideas of sense as passing in and out of existence with every turn of man's attention ; they have represented the ideas as ' generated ' by the act of sense, although Berkeley in terms denies it (§ 90). Such mistakes are fundamental ; any pre-sentation of Berkeley's teaching that embodies them is radically wrong, and completely misrepresents what the historical Berkeley taught. Berkeley took the measure of the problem early in his preparatory studies ; he subordinates it, but does not dodge it ; he deals with it in sections 45–48, and there he explicitly says that inter-mittency and the companion doctrines do *not* follow from his principles. Whoever finds that they do has not found the Berkeley of history. Berkeley's theory of perception has room for the perceivable as well as the perceived, for the *posse percipi* as well as for the *percipi*, for the other side of the moon and for the other side of this page, as well as for the sides we see.

Such is Berkeley's summary account of the object perceived, and thus concludes the first stage of his analysis of the perceptual situation. It is significant that he puts the object before the subject. The object is his first interest, his opening theme. Objectivity is the key-note of the *Principles*. He is no solipsist, nor subjectivist, nor subjective idealist ; his starting-point is not the self, but the " it." Descartes begins with the *cogito, ergo sum,*

[1] See *PC* 802 and my note on No. 52.

Berkeley begins with the *cogitatur, ergo est*.[1] He believed in the sensible world, as you and I do. He looked out on the Dublin mountains, and so do I as I write these words. The world of which those mountains are a part was the great theme of his *New Theory of Vision* and of his *Principles*, and that is why his *magnum opus* opens with this declaration on the ultimate nature of the objects composing that world.

To call this colourful, fragrant, resonant, radiant world of ours " a collection of ideas " sounds strange to modern ears ; but every science is entitled to its own technique ; precision is impossible otherwise. Perceptual analysis has to work in the technique of its own day. Berkeley is studying perception and using the technique of his day. When he styles the things about us " collections of ideas," he is not substituting shadows for reality ; he is simply insisting that sensible things are sensible, purely sensible. This visible, be it shape or colour, *is* visible ; this tangible, be it rough or smooth, *is* tangible ; each, as seen or touched, is " perfectly known " (§ 87). This is not to say that sense perception is the only way of knowing, or that we can find out all there is to things by gawking and gazing at them as cows gawk and gaze at Killarney. Berkeley's system allows full scope to the " other ways of knowing," and to the higher activities of thought ; but while we sense, he urges, let us sense ; let us trust our senses, and set the *sensible* at arm's length ; for the senses can disclose all the sensibility of things, and therefore matter is an otiose conception which clouds the issue and explains nothing.

[1] *i.e.* It is thought ; therefore it is. I am told that the Latin of the phrase is not classical, but that its meaning is clear enough.

CHAPTER IV

THE PERCEIVING SUBJECT

(Principles, § 2)

BERKELEY now gives a succinct, preliminary account of the perceiving subject. He turns from " all that endless variety of ideas or objects of knowledge " to a different order of being, to the " perceiving active being," whose functions are to know and to perceive ideas and to operate about them in will, imagination, memory, etc. He names this being indifferently *mind, spirit, soul,* or *my self.*

The points to be noticed in this section are the description of the subject or mind, the emphatic statement of its distinctness from ideas, and the hint of the New Principle.

Psychology has changed since Berkeley's day ; whether it has changed for the better or the worse posterity must say ; but it has changed. Berkeley's conception of the mind is not quite our conception ; we have something to learn about the mind, and not a little to unlearn, before we can properly understand his famous doctrine of existence in the mind. If readers assume that Berkeley meant by *mind* just what our text-books of psychology mean by it, they will miss the key to the true interpretation of his teaching.

Activity is the essence of Berkeleian mind or subject, rational, percipient activity, and until we form the habit of considering ourselves in that light, we cannot move freely in the Berkeleian system. It is an easy habit to form, springing straight from the facts of life. When I come round after an anaesthetic, I come round to my normal awareness of myself as an active being confronting passive being. I act; I am. But the mind which is the object of introspection in our text-books, the mind which can be divided into three parts or attitudes, is not quite the mind that Berkeley knew. The mind which is the observer only, which sits, as it were, in a touch-line seat, a passive spectator of the game of life, watching the senses function, the memory register, and the will make New Year's resolutions—that is not the mind which Berkeley felt himself to be. The object-mind which is not active subject, the mosaic mind of the mental atomists and the mindless mind of the Freudian unconscious— these conceptions of the mind are remote from Berkeley's. Of the feelings and emotions and all that is to-day classed under the affective attitude he says little. He was not concerned with them; probably he would class them with the functions of the body in large part; he would certainly keep them distinct from the urge and impulse and spontaneity of mind. The mind, for him, is the act and not the states of mind.

He took his views from personal experience, I think, not from books; in the pages of his *Commentaries* [1] we can see him gradually fighting his way towards full self-knowledge; the earlier entries speak of the mind as passive, and identical, or nearly so, with its contents; he can take Hume's viewpoint, and call the mind "a congeries of perceptions" (No. 580); but in the end he reached the position of the *Principles*, in which mind is active and is distinguished from its contents as sharply as active from passive.

Mind, for him, is *a* mind, a being, a thing, a thinking thing, a spirit; it is not an atmosphere, not merely non-

[1] See especially No. 788 and my notes on Nos. 14, 154, and 576.

physical existence ; it is a centre of experience, a centre
which is not its circumference, an *actus* which is not its
states.   It is substance which supports its accidents ; it
is subject which *has* its objects.   This central pulse of
active being can never be an object to mind in the same
way as unthinking things are objects : they are ideas ;
it is not : they are passive ; it is active : we know it,
but we have no idea of it : for an idea, being passive,
cannot represent the activity in which mind consists.
We are *conscious* of the mind, but the attempt to conceive
it by way of idea, *i.e.* to form a mental picture of it, is
as futile as the attempt to touch or see it.

The mind's modes of operation are various ; its
principal activities are understanding and will ; but it
acts also in imagination and sentience.   We are inclined
to picture the eye, for instance, as a camera, and the
mind as a being which watches it work and every now
and then collates its informations and interprets them ;
but there is activity *in* seeing, not only *after* it, and therefore Berkeley could not hand over sentience to the not-
mind.   The mind, for him, works in thought, in the
imagination, and in sense, and that is why he so often
uses the one word " perceive " to cover all those activities.
He would probably grant that in practice we are not
able to delimit the activity of mind with precision, and
yet he would maintain that what we know to be active
in us we know to be mind, and that what we know to be
mind, we know to be active.

This conception of the mind gives a decisive turn to
Berkeley's immaterialism.   Such a subject as he describes
must have its object ; such a perceiving being must have
something to perceive ; such an active being must have
that on which to act ; its sea must find a shore.   The
common notion of Berkeley's world as made of mind-stuff

is completely out. Mind-stuff has no place in his philosophy ; and the concluding sentence of this section makes this clear. The mind, he says, is not " any one of my ideas, but a thing intirely distinct from them." *Intirely distinct*, the words are decisive on this crux of Berkeleian exegesis. When my eye first fell on them, my whole conception of the philosophy began to change. They are set here prominently at the outset, and they are repeated with growing emphasis later in the work. They are incompatible with monist or panpsychist immaterialism, and they mark off Berkeley's immaterialism as a dualist system, under God, of sense and spirit. Berkeley had studied the question long and closely. He hesitated about it in his notebooks ; but once he had made up his mind, and taken his decision, all trace of hesitation left him. Mind is mind, for him, and ideas are ideas, and the twain never merge. Mind is mind, for him, and ideas are not-mind. Mind and ideas, being " intirely distinct," the two are two and are never one. Berkeley's declaration is coupled with his first allusion to existence in the mind, and is all the more impressive on that account. It is as if he meant to warn his readers that they are bound to misunderstand him unless they keep what is in the mind " intirely distinct " from the mind itself.

This distinction is in the ground-plan of the book, in its very fabric (§ 86), and it is hardly necessary to quote passages ; but here they are ; in section 27 we read that " the words *will* [*understanding, mind,* first ed.], *soul, spirit,* do not stand for different ideas, or in truth for any idea at all, but for something which is very different from ideas " ; in section 89 spirits and ideas are stated to be " two kinds intirely distinct and heterogeneous, and which have nothing common but the name [being] " ; in section 142 we are told that " *spirits* and *ideas* are things

so wholly different, that when we say, *they exist, they are
known*, or the like, these words must not be thought to
signifie anything common to both natures.''

There is a broad hint of immaterialism in section 2,
as in section 1 ; for if the mind which is distinct from
the ideas yet *has* the ideas, how can matter *have* them ?
If the mind entertains or perceives the objects of sense,
how can matter entertain or perceive them ?   Try it out
in a concrete case.   I perceive this song ; it is in my
mind ; it is quite distinct from my mind, but it exists
in my mind.   Does it exist also in matter ?   No ; it does
not make sense to say so ; we all know it is not true.
Matter cannot hear the melody, or perceive the song ;
matter has no ears ; it cannot have, entertain, or perceive
an audible object.   I watch the sun set behind the Twelve
Pins of Connemara.   I see yonder crimson and gold and
amber.   They are in my mind.   I am watching them.
What is the sense of saying they exist in matter ?   It is
not true ; for they are in my mind, and I know it.
Matter has no eyes ; matter cannot have, entertain, or
perceive what is there, what I see.   Where light is, there
is no dark ; where mind is, there is no matter.   There
are illuminated things which are not light ; just so there
are sensible things which are not mind ; and that is
what Berkeley teaches in this crucial section.   There is
no matter, but there is the sensible.

The same result meets us when we put together the
results of sections 1 and 2.   The subject is a perceiving
active being ; the object is a collection of ideas.   Those
are the finite factors, according to Berkeley, in any and
every case of sense perception.   The infinite factor has
not yet been mentioned.   Berkeley comes to it all in good
time, and without it his account of the perceptual situation is not complete ; but it is possible to consider per-

ception at the human level without regard to the divine Mind implied in it, and Berkeley undoubtedly does so, and finds it useful, up to a point, to do so. Taking it at that level, then, when a man perceives a thing, an active being is perceiving a group or collection of ideas. That is the situation, and there is no other finite factor. Then there is no need to look for a representation of something not present, and there is no need to look for some ulterior or mediate object ; the immediate object is quite enough ; for in perceiving sensible things, like chairs and tables, the mind directly apprehends those significant entities which Berkeley called ideas and which we call sense data. The collection of ideas or group of sense data is obviously there, and we know it, and in apprehending it we apprehend the sensible thing. But there is no other object, no object of a different kind, and if we postulate a non-significant, non-sensible object as well as the significant data or ideas, if, that is, we postulate matter, we are completely falsifying the situation. In a word, if Berkeley is right about the finite factors in perception, material substance disappears.

The concluding words of the section are, " for the existence of an idea consists in being perceived." This statement is, in slightly disguised form, the New Principle openly announced in section 3. If Berkeley has anything startling to say, it is his custom to introduce it by degrees to the readers' notice, and this innocent-looking statement is here, no doubt, as a shock-absorber for the revolutionary declaration which follows. The New Principle is a statement on the nature of existence. Here its scope is, in word, restricted to " ideas," but in the next section it is stated without that restriction, argued fully, and applied to all sensible things. The restriction is only verbal ; anyone who has mastered the argument of the previous chapter would at once see through the disguise ; for, on Berkeley's showing, sensible things *are* ideas ; there is no difference in kind between them, and what is true of the existence of the idea must be true of the existence of the thing which is composed of ideas. It is a nice little piece of controversial *finesse*, because the average reader, in Berkeley's day and to-day, would find no difficulty in admitting that the existence of an *idea* consists in being perceived ; the shoe pinches only when one is asked to extend that principle to mountains, rivers, etc.

The New Principle is the main topic of the next chapter, and here I need only make a few remarks about it by way of introduction.

The New Principle explains the meaning of the term *existence* as applied to sensible things ; it lays down that existence is existence in the mind ; for *to be* is *to be perceived* ; *esse est percipi*. It is a deep principle, but not a difficult principle, if it is taken in the way I suggest. It is commonly regarded as the *pons asinorum* of the Berkeleian philosophy ; but a great deal of artificial difficulty has been imported into it. It has deep implications about the existent thing and about the mind ; but before trying to master those deeper implications, we should fix our attention on the surface meaning of the words. To exist is to exist in the mind, *i.e.* to be perceived. Berkeley brings it in very simply and naturally, and we ought to take it in the same way. He has been describing his mind ; he says it is a thing in which his ideas exist, *i.e.* (he adds) " whereby they are perceived." There is nothing strange or startling so far ; for " I have an idea of " is just a colloquialism for " I perceive," and what I perceive must exist, and while I perceive it, it must exist in my mind. Thus existence in the mind, cleared of those finicking refinements read into the phrase by modern psychology and idealism, is the most homely and familiar thing, without any mystical or psychic suggestion. If a colour exists in the mind, then the mind perceives it ; if it does not exist in the mind, the mind does not perceive it. We all think and speak that way every day of our lives. When your wife asks you to match a ribbon down town, and adds, "Now, dear, do keep it in mind," she does not mean that either the ribbon or her words are to form an inseparable part of what the psychologist calls your mind. She just wants you to mind it, as she minds the children. And when Berkeley says that sensible things are or exist in the mind, he does not mean that they form part of the perceiving subject ; he has just said the very opposite ; he has just said they are " intirely distinct " from the mind. He means simply that they are objects of attention, like the ribbon or the children. They are in the mind because they are significant objects of cognition or volition. They are not *in* the mind, as Monday is *in* the week, but as a hippopotamus is *in* my mind when I see or imagine him. Existence in the mind is thus existence for the mind, existence as object of the mind, existence in relation to the mind, existence perceived.

Then, too, I must explain the word *only*, which Berkeley often prefixes. When a casual speaker says, That is only in the mind, he means, as we say, That's all in my eye. He means it is a dream or a fancy, gone with the wind or the dreaming. He means that it really does not exist at all. But when Berkeley says, That exists only in the mind, there is nothing depreciatory about the *only* ; it is his slogan, his war-cry, his banner. He means that it exists, but does not exist in matter. The controversial import of this key phrase is often overlooked. " Only in the mind," means " not in matter." The force of the *only* lies in the fact that matterists of Berkeley's day (and of any day if they think out their creed to its consequences) postulated *two* existences for the things of sense, the one existence " intelligible " or in the mind, and the other existence " real," *i.e.* outside the mind in matter.   Against this alleged " twofold existence of the objects of sense " (§ 86) Berkeley was up in arms.[1]   He said that sensible things exist, but that they have only one existence, existence in the mind, and therefore they have no existence in matter.   He affirmed sensible existence, but denied material existence.

[1] We must never forget that the *esse est percipi* converts ; if a thing is perceived, for Berkeley, really perceived, it *eo ipso* exists.

CHAPTER V

THE MEANING OF " EXISTENCE "

(*Principles*, §§ 3–5)

" I wonder not at my sagacity in discovering the obvious tho' amazing truth, I rather wonder at my stupid inadvertency in not finding it out before." [1] In these words Berkeley records his feelings about his discovery of his New Principle. He discovered the meaning of the term *existence*. *He* did not wonder at his sagacity, but we may pause to do so. Let us pay him the tribute of a moment's wonder that a young man, twenty-two years old, could think out for himself a principle so far-reaching in its consequences, so remote from time-honoured ways of thought.

So far Berkeley has described the perceptual situation, and now in the light of his *Heureka* he begins to interpret it. In section 3 he drives home and clinches the arguments of sections 1 and 2 by a new analysis of the meaning of the term *existence*. Thus he reaches " an intuitive knowledge " of the facts. [2] By " intuitive knowledge " he means nothing mystical or praeternatural, but that fully assured knowledge which comes from seeing the situation as it really is, seeing it steadily and seeing it whole. Attend, says Berkeley, to the meaning of the term *exist* as applied to sensible things, and you know intuitively, [3] you *see*, that objects of sense

---

[1] *PC* 279.
[2] Descartes and Locke had described as " intuitive " the knowledge with the highest degree of certainty. Berkeley, no doubt, adopted it from them, but extended it beyond self-knowledge ; see *PC* 547 and my note *ib.*
[3] *Cf. intueor.*

" cannot exist otherwise than in a mind perceiving them."
In other words, focus your attention on the *existence* of
the object perceived, and you reach a close-up view of the
perceptual situation, and you see, as if by direct vision
in broad daylight, that there is no matter.

What is existence ? What do we mean by the term ?
Berkeley replies that the existence of passive, unthinking
things is *to be perceived* (*esse est percipi*), and that the existence
of minds or active things is *to perceive* (*esse est percipere*),
and that therefore existence in general, whether of passive
thing or of active thing, is necessarily related to mind or
spirit.[1] This is " the obvious tho' amazing truth." It
is an amazing truth, if it is true, because thinkers have for
centuries been dragooned into thinking that existence is
just the opposite of perception. We have been drilled
into thinking that there is some state called existence,
which things have or possess, as we have or possess a
five-pound note. We suppose that things " have existence," mere or bare existence, and that subsequently the
eye or mind comes along and perceives them. Don't ask
me what this *existence* is, we say ; for I cannot tell you ;
but don't let us deny it, or the bottom will fall out of
our world.

Yet this vague, traditional notion of existence constantly pulls us up. It does so very markedly at the top
end of the scale. The ontological argument takes existence
as a detachable attribute and discusses whether God
possesses existence as he possesses goodness, wisdom,
power, and the other perfections. That accounts for the

[1] Passive existence receives, as is natural, more attention than active ;
but both parts of the New Principle are axiomatic for Berkeley, and are
often in his mind together ; *e.g. Princ.* § 81, " a notion of entity or existence,
abstracted from spirit and idea, from perceiving and being perceived "
(Fraser reads " perceived " for " perceiving," and makes nonsense of the
passage) ; see also *Three Dialogues*, ii *ad fin*. In *PC* 429 the full Latin
formula is sketched, " Existence is percipi or percipere, or velle i:e. agere."

artificial air of Anselm's argument ; it is to many people a line of thought which leads to Deity, but, strictly, it does not prove what we want proved. By detaching existence from action and the qualities accompanying action, it makes the debate hollow ; for the divine *existentia* or existence can be none other than God's act and thought.

Turn now to the other end of the scale. What do we mean when we assert or deny existence in ordinary life ? The giraffe exists ; the sea serpent does not exist. The giraffe exists. How do you know ? Why, I have seen one in the Zoo. The sea serpent does not exist. How do you know ? Well, I have never seen one, nor met anybody who has seen one. But if a credible witness came along and said he had seen one, we should say then, "Of course it exists." It would seem, so far, that Berkeley is right, and that when we say a thing exists we mean that it is perceived by sense.

But at this stage some one is sure to make a distinction within perception, and say, No ; I mean more than that by sensible existence. When I say, The giraffe exists, I do not so much mean that it is being perceived. I mean rather that it might be perceived, and can cease to be perceived ; and that seems to imply that existence is something other than perception.

Now this answer raises supplementary questions, but does not really traverse Berkeley's answer to the main question. The main question is, What does existence mean in the case of a thing which I am actually perceiving ? For our first concern is to find out whether there is matter in this table I am actually seeing and touching. There are other questions : What does existence mean in the case of a thing I might perceive ? What does it mean in the case of a thing I have perceived and perceive no longer? In due course Berkeley deals with them; but it is a mistake to go off on supplemental questions before one has faced squarely the main question and digested the main answer, *viz.* that *esse est percipi* in the case of what is being actually perceived. If you assert that the giraffe can cease to be perceived, you are implying that it has been perceived, and may be perceived again, and therefore you leave it "still with relation to perception," [1] and you certainly do not assert or imply that it never has been perceived, never will be perceived, and never can be perceived; you do not assert or imply "the absolute existence of unthinking things without any relation to their being perceived." Past existence, future existence, and possible existence are all relative to perception, and *absolute existence* is a mere limbo, an unintelligible concept.

Sooner or later the reader will have to deal with the question, What happens, on Berkeleian principles, to the object we are no longer perceiving? Let it be "later," rather than "sooner." Put it off as long as you can. Berkeley expects the question to be raised, and answers it in outline on this his first mention of the New Principle; but the main issue for him and everybody lies in the factors of *actual* perception. Take care of the percept, and the perceivable will take care of itself. Berkeley's business, first and foremost, is to explain the *esse* of things when they are being actually perceived. He tells us that actual existence is to be actually perceived. If he is wrong, let someone tell us where he is wrong; let someone tell us what is the existence of this sight I see, this sound I hear, over and above my seeing the sight and hearing the sound. Till that is done (and it never has been done), let no one misjudge, misrepresent, or undervalue Berkeley's

[1] *PC* 802, where see my note.

answer just because he cannot explain in one breath or compress into one neat formula all that is meant by actual and possible existence, real and imagined existence, active and passive existence, finite and infinite existence.[1]

In point of fact the *esse est percipi* is an elastic principle, meant to stretch ; it can cover the thought-form or existence-form under examination. Berkeley himself extends it to cover active existence, saying, " existence is percipi or percipere, or velle i:e. agere." [2] In section 23 he argues that imagined existence is imagined perception, which accords with the explicit and inclusive statement in his *Commentaries*.[3] When, therefore, we are dealing with the perceivable, not actually being perceived by you or me, we are fully entitled to explain possible existence as possible perception. Berkeley does so, in effect, and his formula for passive existence thus expands naturally into *esse est percipi aut posse percipi*.

Now let us refer to the all-important passage in the *Principles* (§ 3) and work through it sentence by sentence. Berkeley starts from " what every body will allow," *viz.* that thoughts, feelings, and ideas of the imagination do not exist without the mind. I think of a law of nature ; I feel angry ; I imagine Hamlet. The three objects are experienced ; the law, the anger, Hamlet, *exist*, or they could not be experienced ; they exist in my mind, and they exist there in different ways, each in its appropriate way ; but they exist. What, then, is this *existence* universally attributed to such objects ? There can only be one answer. *Existence* means to be experienced, to be in the

---

[1] On existence in space and time, see below, p. 63.

[2] *PC* 429.

[3] " The existence of our ideas consists in being perceiv'd, imagin'd thought on . . . it must be well noted that existence is vulgarly restrain'd to actuall perception. & that I use the word Existence in a larger sense than ordinary." *PC* 472-73, where see my note.

mind; that is, to be an object of the mind.   That is what existence means in these three cases ; that is all it means. The law is conceived ; the anger is felt ; the Prince of Denmark is imagined.

The same holds, says Berkeley, of sense perception. Here he was consciously the pioneer, " voyaging strange seas of thought, alone."   " To me," he says, " it is no less evident that the various sensations or ideas imprinted on the sense, however blended or combined together (that is, whatever objects they compose) cannot exist otherwise than in a mind perceiving them."   To be sure of this you have only to attend, he claims, to the meaning of the term *exist* when it is applied to sensible things.   Then, as his manner is, he takes us straight to the concrete case, " The table I write on, I say, exists, *i.e.* I see and feel it, . . ." The nerve of Berkeley's philosophy, perhaps his central contribution to world thought, is in that " *i.e.*" ; so let us take him up rightly and be sure that we grasp exactly what he has said.   He has not said that I make the table by seeing and feeling it ; he has not said that the table *is* my subjective act of seeing and feeling.   He is explaining the meaning of the term *existence* ; and he says that the table's *existence* is nothing over and above its being seen and felt.   There is not a table seen and felt *and* a table existing.   If someone says, " The table does not exist," I reply, " Yes, it does.   I see and feel it."

The existence of matter is here at issue ; in denying to the table any existence other than perceived existence, Berkeley is denying so-called material existence.   He is not denying body ; he is not denying the table ; his elbow was resting on the table as he wrote.   He is asserting sensed existence and with it sensible existence, but he is denying this non-sensed, non-sensible, nonsensical existence, called material, saying, in effect, that there simply is not room for it, and that the term has no meaning in view of the facts of the situation.

Some may think that space and time provide a loop-hole for the matterist. They may try to vivify this lifeless phrase (" material existence ") by identifying it with existence in space and time ; but concrete thinking dis-poses of this loophole in a moment. All sensible existence is existence in space and time. Berkeley's table was some-where and of some period ; and to say that the table is in space and time does not take it out of the range of the senses and the mind, but simply sets it in its spatio-temporal context, and asserts its two-way continuity with other sensible things. Existence in space and time is just another name for sensible existence ; for all concrete space and time is sensible.

Turn now from actual perception to possible percep-tion, and consider Berkeley's preliminary pronouncement about it. We must go back to the comma at which we broke off. Here is the rest of the interrupted sentence about the table : " and if I were out of my study I should say it existed, meaning thereby that if I was in my study I might perceive it, or that some other spirit actually does perceive it." To be is to be perceived ; then if it is not perceived, has it no existence ? What happens to your study table, Berkeley, when you go out for a walk ? Does it still exist ? Yes, he replies, unequivocally, " I should say it existed."

Countless jokes at Berkeley's expense fall flat in view of that reply. " I should say it existed "—whatever con-struction is to be placed on the words, there is one thing they cannot mean, *viz.* I should *deny* it existed. Berkeley is commonly accused of holding that things cease to be when they cease to be sensed. Yet, here, on the first occurrence of the problem he says the very opposite. He says categorically that his table exists when he is not there to see and touch it. In intention, at least, his opinions do not conflict with common sense ; his words, whatever he means by them, tally with common speech.

He tells us what he means by them without beating about the bush, and his explanation, brief as it is, is reasonable and consistent with the *esse est percipi*. He gives a sufficient account of the perceivable without recourse to matter. He means two things (they might both be true in a given case), he says, or one of two things ; he means conditional perception by myself or actual perception by someone else ; he means that " If I was in my study I might perceive it, or that some other spirit actually does perceive it." In either case " *it* " is there ; his furniture is safe ; his table exists in his absence as in his presence ; and what Berkeley means by the words " it exists " is what we all mean, and is all that we mean if only we knew the meaning of our common words. The table exists ; on my return from my walk I shall see it. The table exists ; my skip [1] is dusting it. The table exists when I am out, or it would not be so dustless and disturbed on my return. Its existence is not " absolute " ; that word means nothing here ; its existence is perceived existence, or perceivable existence ; in either case it is " still with relation to perception." [2] Thus Berkeley saves his New Principle and his common sense ; he avoids the doctrine of intermittency with the doctrines which go with it, annihilation and perpetual re-creation [3] ; he retains the unsensed *sensibile* without falling back on the absolute existence demanded by the theory of matter.

---

[1] The traditional term in T.C.D. for a college servant.
[2] *PC* 802.
[3] See §§ 45–48 with my discussion on p. 121*ff*.

The rest of section 3 applies the New Principle to the several constituents of the sensible thing, enshrines it in a Latin formula, and thus commends it to the learned world.

Tables have constituents. The Berkeleian table is made up of the immediate objects of the senses, colours, touches, smells, etc., which, collected together and marked by one name, constitute the thing (§ 1). Accordingly Berkeley proceeds to apply his teaching to the constituents of the thing. " There was an odour." What does the word *was* mean there ? What is the *existence* of the smell ? The existence of the smell is the perception of the smell. Was there a smell ? Yes, I smelt it, or it was smelt. The same holds of the proper objects of the other senses. Hearing, sight, and touch are mentioned. " There was a sound, *i.e.* it was heard ; a colour or figure, and it was perceived by sight or touch." The stress on the object should be noted : *it* was smelt, *it* was heard, *it* was perceived. Berkeley does not equate " there was a smell " with " there was a smelling," or " there was a sound " with " there was a hearing." He is no subjective idealist ; he does not say or hold that my smelling is the smell or makes it, or that my hearing is the sound or makes it ; for him, the smell is the smell and the sound is the sound ; but the *existence* of smell and sound are, he insists, nothing other than the smell smelt and the sound heard. Their existence is thus essentially relative to mind ; for smells are to be smelt, and sounds are to be heard. That is their nature ; they are significant things, meant for sentience, meant for mind, like a, b, c, and d. Their alleged material or absolute existence without " any relation to their being perceived " has thus been shown to be " perfectly unintelligible."

Esse est percipi. This far-reaching principle was, in its

first promulgation, an audacious flight of inventive genius. But, once announced, it is seen to be inevitable by those who will deal fairly with it ; for it is common sense and speculative truth. Perhaps never before in the history of philosophy has so much new truth been said in so few or so simple words. Existence, *existentia*, a standing-out against a background—write the term in English, write it in Latin, or in any other tongue ; write it in capitals, or in small ; apply it to sensible things or to supersensible ; in all cases the term adds nothing to the object of thought or sense, and only adds a pale and watery stress to the mind-form used. If I see a horse, I see it existing. If I imagine a unicorn, I imagine it existing. If I believe in myself, I believe in my existence. If I believe in God or worship Him, I believe in His existence and worship Him that is.

In sections 4 and 5 Berkeley neatly works into his argument the results of his Introduction. His theory has exposed and refuted the " second " existence of sensible things, retaining their sense-given existence, but abolishing their so-called " natural or real [existence], distinct from their being perceived." It all looks so simple to him, and he wonders why others do not see it so. Why do they hold on to this "opinion strangely prevailing amongst men " which leads to " a manifest contradiction," *viz.* an insensible object of sense." Why should there be this clash of opinion about something so close to us ? Why should the existence of matter appear obvious to others, absurd to him ? The doctrine of abstraction makes all the difference. He thinks in the concrete, the others think in the abstract. They are slaves of abstract ideas ; he is emancipated. On the abstract idea of *existence* this particular issue turns. Others abstract the existence of a smell from its being smelt ; they abstract the existence of a sound from its being heard, and they claim to have framed the abstract general idea of existence. You might as well abstract and separate a thing from itself ; you might as well make existence exist, and walking walk.

Does he then deny abstraction *in toto* ? No. He can conceive separately things that can exist or be perceived asunder, such as milk without cream, a body without legs and arms, or a rose without a thorn or scent ; if that is all that is meant by abstraction, of course he can abstract.[1] For that simply means that he can isolate in thought, can form partial mental images, can imagine the relevant in detachment from the irrelevant. But he cannot form Locke's abstract general ideas ; he cannot, even in thought, separate the inseparable, *e.g.* motion from the moving body, the sight from the thing seen, existence from perception, *esse* from *percipi*.

This attack on abstraction with the qualification which Berkeley habitually adds is simply a résumé of the argument of the Introduction.[2] It is not a decisive, positive, direct argument against matter, nor is it advanced as such ; but it is a solid explanation of the prevalence of the traditional belief in matter amongst those who have reached the middle levels of speculative thought.

[1] See *Principles*, Introduction, § 10, and p. 36 above. [2] See Chapter II.

CHAPTER VI

GOD AND HUMAN PERCEPTION

(Principles, §§ 6 and 7)

BERKELEY here completes his account of the perceptual situation with a brief but impressive reference to the divine factor. The brevity and restraint of the passage have given some readers the impression that Berkeley is not very much in earnest about it. Some expositors have declared that God is an afterthought in the Berkeleian philosophy, a buttress for a tottering metaphysic, a *deus ex machina* dragged in to save a collapsing theory of perception, originally conceived in terms of human psychology.

Now Berkeley was frankly interested in the manner of our perceiving, and he had specialized in the psychology of vision. He considered that a philosophical study of sight is sufficient to refute many of the arguments for matter. Hence he is prepared to go a long way in his discussion with scarcely a mention of God. But that is not to say that in its original design and conception his immaterialism was without a God. In his own index of the entries in his *Commentaries* there is G for God, as well as M for matter ; and if you study the entries, both those with the marginal sign G and others, you find not alone piety, but a metaphysic built on God and God in the ground-plan of the metaphysic. This work, a study preliminary to the writing of his two great books, opens with notes on eternity ; on its fourth page is forecast

" a direct & brief demonstration of an active powerfull being distinct from us on whom we depend " (No. 41). Matter is set forth as an anti-God (Nos. 290, 298, 310, 625). God is creator (No. 60), and nature his " ordinance " (No. 794). God is universal cause (Nos. 433, 780), and man is powerless without Him (No. 107) ; God is the substance of our ideas (No. 109) and my sensations demonstrate His being (No. 838) ; God is all-comprehending and all-encompassing (Nos. 348, 675, 812, 827). That theology bears the distinctive marks of Berkeley's metaphysic, and his metaphysic bears the distinctive marks of that theology ; for the metaphysic and the theology are one and the same *theoria* which had been working like leaven in Berkeley's intellect some years before he went to press.[1]

Berkeley's reticence about God is conscious art ; he unfolds his theology gradually. You think he is building a house ; you find he has built a church. Had he said all at once all he had to say about God, readers would have thought his work a trite theological disquisition, and might have missed its novel, philosophical contentions. He wanted to show that matter drugs the theistic impulse ; he wanted to set God forth as substance, as cause, and as the " place of spirits " ; " the main drift and design " of his labours (§ 156) was to show that we depend absolutely and immediately upon God. But he could not attempt to explain all that at the outset, and, wisely, he took the other path, and allows his full doctrine of deity to dawn slowly on his readers' minds. In section 6 the notion of God as sole substance is introduced allusively,

[1] It is scarcely necessary to labour the point, but if further proof is desired, I refer readers to the *New Theory of Vision*, where the argument culminates in the conception of the visible world as divine visual language. Substitute *sensible* for *visible*, and you reach the fundamental conception of the *Principles*.

almost hypothetically [1] ; in sections 29–33 God is shown as cause, as the source of real ideas, and as the Lord of nature, and in sections 45–48 as the home of the perceivable ; in sections 145 ff. Berkeley rises to the full height of his argument, and sets forth the manner of man's knowledge of God in passages of rare beauty and sustained dignity, passages remarkable for their depth of thought and feeling, for their clarity and simple sincerity.

Consider section 6. Here, we are told, is a " near and obvious " truth. Berkeley was fond of the phrase. In his *Commentaries* (Nos. 270, 279) the New Principle is an " obvious truth " ; in his *Principles* (§ 149) the existence of God is a " near and obvious " truth ; and in the passage before us the same term is skilfully made to apply both to the New Principle and to the existence of God ; for the reader is insensibly led on from existence in the mind of man to existence in the mind of the eternal spirit. The one opens into the other as bud into flower. The omnipresence of the all-operative spirit is a corollary of the New Principle ; it is the *esse est percipi* raised to a higher power, raised to infinity.

Take perception first on the human level ; consider the " furniture of the earth," the things we see about us, the sense data we perceive on the horizontal plane ; these imply my mind ; they involve it ; the objects of my actual perception are actually within my mind, and have their existence there. Then raise the eye ; look up to " the choir of heaven " ; comprehend in one view both heaven and earth ; view in one conspect " all those bodies which compose the mighty frame of the world " ; pass in thought from my microcosm to God's macrocosm ;

[1] But the language is lofty and obviously studied. It is interesting to observe how Berkeley has expanded and decorated this passage, and made it into the glittering account of nature at the opening of the second of the *Three Dialogues*.

see the total perceptual situation in its full length and
breadth and height. It is " a near and obvious truth "
that universal, eternal Mind is demanded, mind that
matches its effects. As my small world implies my mind,
so does the universal system of sensible things imply the
mind of God. In both worlds the object is not absolute,
but relative to mind, and therefore the elements of heaven
and earth, the a, b, c, d of all created things, when I am
not seeing them and you are not seeing them, must either
have no existence at all (which is absurd, Berkeley implies)
or they must subsist (*i.e.* have their substance) " in the
mind of some eternal spirit." " Some eternal spirit "
—the phrase is vague and unconventional, but the argument behind it is closely knit. The unconventionality is
part of Berkeley's art ; he wishes to lead men by new
paths to the old truths.

It is clear that God, to Berkeley, was no " asylum of
ignorance," no remote inference, no *ex machina* device
giving a verbal solution to the problem of the perceivable,
but a positive, rational, and inevitable principle, his
starting-point. God is ; can there be matter ? In the
spirit of that question he approached his problems.

In that spirit his immaterialism should be approached
to-day. It is possible to believe both in God and in matter,
but it is not easy to do so. The two beliefs where they are
held together remain in a state of uneasy equilibrium ; it
is very hard to hold both beliefs together intelligently and
firmly. In conjunction they are not a natural deliverance
of experience. I think the history of the notion of matter
bears out this contention. The ancient Greeks worked
out the notion of matter because they had no usable notion
of deity. They philosophized first in Ionia, it is said,
because no priests were there. Thinking men could not
believe in the gods many of the official creed ; they had

no taste for the mystery religions, and, instead, they
sought to find the *nature* of things, the φύσις, the substance, without recourse to deity.   When Thales said
that all was water, he was abstracting from the sensible,
and thought was moving towards matter ;   the opposite
movement towards form found itself in Pythagoras and
Plato.   Aristotle combined the two movements, and gave
them classical expression in his composite doctrine of form
and matter, which is enshrined, or rather embalmed, in
our language and ways of thought.   History thus supplies
support for Berkeley's challenge :

> "Matter once allow'd.   I defy any man to prove that God is
> is not matter." [1]

The atheist having no other principle for explaining
sight and touch and the cause of change has to postulate
matter.   For him it is a case of : If there is no matter,
il faut l'inventer.   On the other hand, the attempt to retain
effective belief in both principles gives rise to great
difficulties ;   in practice, the one principle or the other
is lost to sight ;   for no man can serve these two masters,
and whoever tries to do so must be for ever asking himself,
God is ;   can there be matter ?   or, Matter is ;   can there
be God ?

Of course there are theists who believe in matter, and
there are matterists who believe in God.   But are there
many who believe effectively, clearly, and consciously
in both ?   No thinker can serve these two masters well.
All philosophers, or almost all, admit that the surface
of things, though real, is not enough, and that the outward show, a real appearance, points beyond itself ;
and once in a lifetime we spread the wings of speculative
thought and make one grand assumption.   Two such

[1] *PC* 625

flights are rarely made ; two grand assumptions, like spiritual substance and material substance, are not consistent. Berkeley's challenge forces the issue and compels decision. What is to be the character of our master-assumption ? Is it to be a great Unknowable, like matter, or a great Knowable like universal mind and spirit, an unknown God in a measure known ? The *Principles* asks that fundamental question.

Berkeley's intellectual history points in the same direction. Being a member of the Church of Ireland, he was brought up in the belief that God is everywhere and works all, in all. When he was of age to think for himself, he found that teaching powerfully set forth in Malebranche's philosophy.[1] He refused much that Malebranche taught ; he objected to his representationism, to his abstractionism, to his occasionalism and his matterism. He was too original a thinker to be a Malebranchian, or, for the matter of that, a Lockian ; but to deny that during his plastic period he came strongly under the influence of the Oratorian is to fly in the face of the facts, and to flout the judgement of his contemporaries and his own tacit admission. Malebranche had retained the name and the ghost of matter for ecclesiastical reasons [2] ; but he brought God into immediate, operative contact with the world of sense and with the society of minds. He made his own and set in the forefront of his philosophy the Pauline principle, In Him we live and move and have our being. In that principle Malebranche and Berkeley are at one ; in spite of the wide divergence of their systems the two thinkers meet here. Malebranche was far from pantheism ; Berkeley was further still. Seeing all things in God is incompatible with seeing that God is all things ;

[1] See my *Berkeley and Malebranche*, 1934.
[2] Sir W. Hamilton, Note P, appended to Reid's *Works*.

but there is no great difference in principle between seeing all things in God and seeing all things in the mind. Berkeley, coming to the problem of matter fresh from a study of the *Recherche de la Vérité*, and reacting strongly against much of Locke's teaching, could not have used the phrase " existence in the mind " in a purely psychological or Lockian sense. He saw the visible world as a divine visual language [1]; he had translated the doctrine of the Logos into a philosophic faith. Long before he penned a line of the *Principles* he was convinced that God is the universal cause, present everywhere, acting directly. The full consequences of his panentheism came to him gradually, no doubt ; like all thinkers he took his problems as they arose. We can admit that ; but we must refuse to admit that Berkeley thought of efficacious deity only when his immaterialism was on the verge of a breakdown. The universal Mind in whom we live and move and think could be no afterthought to such a thinker. God was his first thought, his *prius in ordine cognoscendi*, and from that angle, the theological angle, his full doctrine of existence in the mind must be approached, and in the light of that principle it must be interpreted.

A full account of God in the Berkeleian philosophy would be a full account of that philosophy [2] ; and I must confine myself to the question, What does Berkeley mean here by saying that bodies subsist in the mind of God ? We look up at the heavens on a starry night, and say, Yes ; surely there is a God. But to say that Orion and the Pleiades subsist or exist in his mind seems far-fetched and unnecessary. They seem to us to exist " on their

---

[1] *New Theory of Vision*, § 147.
[2] The crucial theological passages in the *Principles* are §§ 29–33, and 146*ff*. ; see below, pp. 150–54.

own." But think again. Will that phrase " exist on their own " really bear analysis in a cool hour ? If Berkeley is right, it is a meaningless phrase, springing from a false abstraction. If Berkeley is right, Orion and the Pleiades, whether considered as points of twinkling light or as celestial balls, or as vast whorls of flaming gas, are essentially significant, bearing an indefeasible, inalienable relation to mind, and the persistent attempts of the human mind to think away their meaning, and to resolve them, in thought, into *meaningless* atoms or similar entities, barely existing, are suicidal. They subsist in the mind of God, because He thought and thinks them, willed and wills them, created and conserves them, orders them, and has set them for signs. To his act and will and thought and law they owe their permanence, their subsistence, from night to night, from age to age, whether they are actually perceived by man or no. A " lost Pleiad " is a loss to man's perception of " the flight of doves," but is no casualty in God's host. To say, then, that bodies subsist in the mind of God is to say that God is the home of the perceivable when it is unperceived by man. The Berkeleian God is thus the background of all that you and I perceive by sense.

But He is in the foreground, too ; and we must carry our analysis a step farther. To subsist in the mind of God is to have an active substance, a substance that acts ; and Berkeley conceives God as taking an active part in human perception. Berkeley thinks that if there were no God, there would be nothing to see or touch ; if we could open our eyes or stretch out our hand, it would be all dark and void. He does not put it in that negative way which sounds a little absurd, the absurdity consisting in the supposition of there being no God. He rather puts it to us that the things we actually see and touch are of such a character that we are bound to infer that God gives them to us. He puts it to us that our actual objects of sense are " ideas " over which we have virtually no control ; we are bound to infer that a wise Spirit produces them and offers them to us. If I come into my lecture room, and see a word or even a letter written on the blackboard, I say, " Hello, who's been here ? " just as Crusoe did when he saw the footprint in the sand. Similarly these significant entities we see and touch, these " ideas " we neither make nor unmake, speak to us of God and his act.

Sunday-school conceptions of deity fail us here, of course ; we must not picture the Berkeleian God in the likeness of man ; we must not think of him as a spasmodic agent, now attending to my wants and now to yours. We must think of the mind of a Shakespeare expressing itself in every syllable and every letter of a hundred plays. We must think of the will of a great leader keeping a million soldiers at their posts and a million workers at their benches, embodying and fixing the collective resolves of a nation. We must think of an all-pervasive, intelligent, beneficent continuous activity, springing from one source.

Produce, *imprint*, and *excite* are Berkeley's chief terms for the modes of the divine activity. God produces ideas of sense for us, imprints them on us, and excites them in us. *Imprint* has a special reference to the significant character of sensible things, and points to Berkeley's metaphor (which is more than a metaphor) of the sensible world as divine language. *Excite* expresses the inward aspect of sense perception. God excites ideas in us, because he enables us to sense what He has produced. Our perceiving is *our* perceiving ; for we are no automata or machines. I open my eyes and perhaps fix my gaze ; but I do not make myself see. I do not know how to do so ; nor does the wisest oculist ; our perceiving is *non sine numine dei*, and the so-called " unconscious action " of the sentient or the sense organs is just a term for the unrecognized act of God.

I need hardly add that, of course, Berkeley is here giving answers to ultimate questions. Sentience may be regarded and studied from other angles ; and for proximate purposes the Berkeleian can quite consistently regard the sense datum from the psychological or the physiological angle, and can accept the facts accepted by the corresponding sciences. The Berkeleian theory is for all at all times ; but the Berkeleian language, as he himself admits (§ 51) is not always in place. The sense of givenness, to which he is here appealing, comes mostly with detachment from the bustle and strain of the working day ; it comes when we are still, and know that God is, when we watch Atlantic breakers or the starry heavens, when we see the day dawn, or the may-fly leave its shuck on the waters of the lake.

CHAPTER VII

ON PICTURES [1] OF MATTER

(*Principles*, §§ 8–21)

IN the first seven sections Berkeley has outlined his case against matter. He has yet to fill in some details—which he does by giving a fuller treatment of existence (§§ 22–24), a discussion of cause (§§ 25–29), and a discussion of the real and the imaginary (§§ 30–33). But first he turns aside to dispose of certain arguments for matter which were used in his day and are silently influential still. Likeness is the principal issue ; hence the title of this chapter. Can it be that our immediate objects are not matter, but are *like* matter ? Can it be that we do not perceive matter itself, but do perceive pictures of matter ? Berkeley disposes of the likeness argument, whether used of primary qualities or of secondary (§§ 8–15). He then carries the war into the opposite camp, maintaining that the term " material substance " is meaningless, that if matter existed, *ex hypothesi* we could not know it, and that the supposition of matter has given rise to unnecessary and trivial disputes both in philosophy and religion (§§ 16–21).

Do we see and touch pictures of matter ? Are the objects we immediately perceive by sense, or any privileged class of them, resemblances, copies, or representations. of that elusive " something we know not what." The matterist says, Yes ; Berkeley says, No. The matterist

---

[1] " It seems then you will have our ideas, which alone are immediately perceived, to be pictures of external things . . .? " *Three Dialogues*, i, *ad fin.*

who is careful of his terms admits that, strictly, we do not perceive matter ; but he affirms that we perceive something like it. Pressed on the point, and asked if there is anything like colour in matter, he usually takes refuge in the famous distinction between primary and secondary qualities. The qualities properly sensible were called by Locke " secondary," *viz*. colour, roughness, softness, taste, sound, smell, etc. The " mathematical " or " primary " qualities were, for the Cartesians, extension, figure, and motion ; and to these Locke added solidity and some others. It was customary to maintain that the primary qualities, or our ideas of them, were like matter, but that the secondary qualities exist only in the mind, *i.e.* only when apprehended, and therefore bear no resemblance to matter. By aid of this distinction the matterist tries to rebut the charge of obscurantism. Matter is, by definition, " something we know not what," and is therefore, to all intents and purposes, irrelevant to perception. Tell the matterist he is putting his faith in he knows not what and he knows not why, and he replies that if he does not know what matter is, he knows what it is like ; it is like extension, if it is not like colour ; it is like solidity, if it is not like sound.

Berkeley first deals with the *likeness* question *per se*. He says, " An idea can be like nothing but an idea." An " idea " for him is an object known or knowable. The idea in question may be an idea of sense or an idea of the imagination ; in either case it cannot be *like* what is unknown and unknowable ; it cannot be like matter. Therefore pictures of matter are impossible. You cannot photograph what is always in the dark. You cannot make a copy or a likeness of " something we know not what." Two things cannot be known to be alike unless they can be compared ; [1] matter and ideas, or, as we should say, matter and sense data, cannot be compared, and therefore they cannot be known to be alike. Sense data are perceivable ; matter is not perceivable.

But is it true that matter is unperceivable ? Dr. Johnson " refuted " Berkeley by kicking a stone in the presence of Boswell. Surely they both perceived the stone he kicked ? [2]

They did, and for that very reason the stone is not matter. Or, if you insist on calling it matter, you are applying the term to what Berkeley called sensible things or ideas of sense. That usage is incorrect, but it is quite common, and Berkeley has it in mind in the dilemma propounded in section 8 ; " I ask whether those supposed originals or external things, of which our ideas are the pictures or representations, be themselves perceivable or no ? " If you answer, Yes, matter is perceivable, then your matter is just a learned name for sensible things ; it is homogeneous with the objects perceived, and of course it is like them ; it is, in Berkeley's terminology, an idea. If, on the other hand, you answer, No, matter is not perceivable, then you must be prepared to take the consequences of your No. Unperceivable matter can have no property cognisable by the senses ; it is not visible, nor tangible, nor audible. Such matter could not possibly be *like* a colour, or a sound, or a roughness. To sum up, matter is either perceivable or unperceivable ; if it is perceivable, it is only another name for the sensible, and is not matter ; it is not material substance. But if it is not perceivable, it is in essence unlike what is perceivable ; therefore no pictures of matter are possible.

[1] See *PC* 378 and my note *ib*.
[2] Professor Jessop aptly says that Johnson kicked the stone, but missed the point.

At this point the distinction between primary and secondary qualities comes in sight. The matterist admits the partial truth of Berkeley's argument. He grants that the secondary qualities are in the mind, and are therefore not like matter ; but primary qualities, he says, are different ; *they* are outside the mind ; we have ideas of them which resemble them.[1] Berkeley gives a comprehensive answer in sections 10–11, and a more detailed answer in sections 12–15. He first points out that the definition of matter thus reached rests on a false abstraction. We are told that matter is " an inert senseless substance in which extension, figure, motion, etc. do actually subsist." But primary qualities cannot be abstracted from secondary ; in the concrete the two are inseparable ; extension is coloured extension ; colour is a colour patch of a certain shape and size ; motion is the movement of a coloured body possessing not only colour but other secondary qualities. The supposed distinction in kind between the two classes cannot be sustained. You cannot make the one class real and material and the other mere appearance. Sauce for the goose is sauce for the gander. If colour, sound, taste, etc., are in the mind, so also are extension, figure, and motion. If the former class cannot furnish pictures of matter, no more can the latter class.

Berkeley then takes the so-called primary qualities one by one, and shows that each is relative to mind. Extension must be great or small ; motion must be swift or slow ; but *great, small, swift,* and *slow* are relative to mind, and are meaningless apart from the mind. Solidity,

[1] " Ideas of primary qualities are resemblances ; of secondary, not." Locke, *Essay*, II viii 15. This is the view of those who hold that if mankind and all other sentient beings disappeared, colours, tastes, scents, sounds, etc., would cease to be, but that solid extended things, with shape, size. number, and motion would remain.

Locke's pet quality, goes into the mind along with extension, for all solidity is extended. Number is "visibly relative," for one yard is three feet and thirty-six inches. The same extension is one, three, and thirty-six, and the number you select for it depends on the uses and purposes of the mind. Unity, which according to Locke (II vii 7) is a simple idea "suggested to the understanding by every object without and every idea within," is an abstract idea to which nothing in reality corresponds.

Thus both by comprehensive survey and by detailed analysis the prerogative claimed for primary qualities has been exploded. The distinction in kind cannot be sustained, and with its disappearance disappears the matterist's plea for pictures of matter like the primary qualities, unlike the secondary qualities.

In sections 14 and 15 Berkeley has a note on the employment of the distinction between primary and secondary qualities as an argument for immaterialism. He is aware that the distinction can be used *against* matter as well as *for* matter. It can be used *ad hominem* against Cartesians and Lockians who used the relativity arguments to prove secondary qualities in the mind, but failed to see that those arguments prove the same of primary qualities. Berkeley himself rests little or nothing on "this method of arguing," and he contrasts it unfavourably with his "arguments foregoing." This *argumentum ad hominem* was, in fact, his old principle [1] which he discarded when he came on his New Principle, or argument from the nature of existence itself.

Berkeley then passes to the counter-offensive, and in sections 16–21 he points out three difficulties in the hypothesis of matter which amount to supplementary argu-

[1] " My first arguings," *PC* 265, where see my note.

ments against it. They are (1) It is hard to assign any intelligible meaning to the term *material substance.* (2) If matter existed, *ex hypothesi,* we could not know it. (3) The conception of matter is the source of disputes in philosophy and religion.

" I have no idea of matter, and therefore cannot explain it." That agnostic defence of matter is still put forward ; the obscure thought is traded as a profound thought. Berkeley urges that matterists ought to have at least " a relative idea of matter " ; if they cannot say what it *is,* they should be able to tell us what it *does* and what purpose it serves. In particular they ought to be able to throw some light on the mysterious cliché, " matter supports accidents." If the term *support* is not to be taken in a literal sense, as when pillars support a roof, in what sense is it to be taken ?

" The most accurate philosophers " declare that by material substance they mean " the idea of being in general together with the relative notion of its supporting accidents." Berkeley urges that the idea of being in general is the most abstract and incomprehensible of all, and that to speak of its supporting accidents is to use words without a meaning. Therefore it is plain to him that matterists do not know what material substance is.

Berkeley goes further and maintains that they cannot know. If they knew, they would have to know it either by sense or by reason. Sense, clearly, cannot enable us to know the non-sensible. Can reason do so ? Given ideas of sense or sense data, can we infer matter from them ? No, says Berkeley ; for there is no necessary connection between ideas in the mind and things outside the mind, as is proved by dreams and frenzies. If we cannot infer external things from ideas that come in sleep, we cannot infer them from waking ideas.

Nor is it true to say that matter is the simplest hypothesis. Matter explains nothing. No matterist attempts to explain *how* ideas are produced, nor *how* body can act upon spirit. For the theist matter is the reverse of explanatory. A theist who believes in matter has to suppose that " God has created innumerable beings [*i.e.* material things] that are intirely useless and serve to no manner of purpose."

Finally (§ 21) Berkeley claims that there are many arguments *a posteriori* against matter ; for matter has given rise to barren controversies in philosophy and to impieties in religion. Later in the book he develops this line of argument, making matter the cause of atheism (§ 92), of fatalism and the denial of immortality (§ 93), of Socinianism (§ 95), of scepticism (§ 92), of geometrical paradoxes and mathematical subtleties (§ 123), of disputes about time (§ 98), about space (§ 123), about real essence (§ 102), about pure space (§ 117), and about fluxions (§§ 130*ff.*). A summary of the *a posteriori* arguments against matter is given in sections 133–34.

CHAPTER VIII

THE ALLEGED BERKELEIAN "CIRCLE"

(*Principles*, §§ 22–24)

" WHEN we do our utmost to conceive the existence of external bodies, we are all the while only contemplating our own ideas. But the mind, taking no notice of itself, is deluded to think it can and does conceive bodies existing unthought of or without the mind ; thô at the same time they are apprehended by or exist in itself."

This passage has been taken to mean that my act of thinking so conditions what I think of that I can never get outside the circle of my own ideas, that my conceiving makes my concepts, and that my world is therefore the product of my mind ; my thinking makes it so. I think of it ; therefore it is thought. I think of it ; therefore it *is*. I am the centre ; my ideas are the circumference. Therefore I and my ideas make up the circle of being, the great circle in which my life is cast. But, it is urged, in the above reasoning the transition from " I think of it ; therefore it is thought " to " I think of it ; therefore it is " is illegitimate and fallacious ; it begs the question, and presupposes what is required to be proved. If, therefore, the Berkeleian circle of being ultimately derives from a circle in argument, Berkeley's immaterialism rests on an elementary mistake in logic, and is founded on the sand.

My aim in this chapter is to show that too much has been read into this passage, that Berkeley's words and thought here are really quite simple, and ought not to be taken in a sophisticated sense. He is not arguing in a circle, nor is he arguing for a circle. The Berkeleian

" circle of being " and Berkeley's " circle in reasoning "
are pure inventions, fathered on him by the idealist
movement.

It has not hitherto been noticed that while section 22
deals with sensible existence, section 23 deals with
imagined existence. Missing this distinction, critics have
missed the thread of the argument. Berkeley has returned
to the meaning of existence,[1] stressing the sufficiency of
his former argument. What is meant by *existence* ? he
asks. In section 22 Berkeley takes the question with
regard to objects of sense, and replies that their existence
is perceived existence, existence in the mind. In section 23
he turns to the imagination. What is meant by *existence*
as applied to objects of the imagination ? In what sense
do imagined trees and books *exist*. He replies that their
existence, too, is existence in the mind ; for it is imagined
perception. In section 24 he draws the conclusion that
since we cannot see or touch *absolute existence*, and cannot
even imagine it, " the absolute existence of unthinking
things are words without a meaning, or which include a
contradiction."

There is no circle in that reasoning. Berkeley has
argued that sensible existence is perceived existence, that
imagined existence is perceived existence imagined, and
that therefore all existence is relative to mind and absolute
existence is an empty form of words. If you see a thing,
you see it existing ; if you imagine a thing, you imagine
it existing. On the score of existence the two faculties
agree, though in other respects they are far apart. The
attempt is often made to give sense perception a monopoly,
and to make existence and sensible existence synonymous ;
but the attempt is based, Berkeley holds, on wrong
psychology.

[1] See Chapter V.

Let us now consider these sections in greater detail. Berkeley has promised a lightning demonstration of immaterialism (" in a line or two "). There is no need to labour the proof ; for the very notion of material exist-ence can be shown to be a contradiction. Look into your own thoughts, he says, and try whether you can conceive it possible for a sound, etc., to exist unperceived. It is a fair challenge. I, for one, have taken it up. I have asked myself the question, Can I conceive a sound exist-ing unperceived ? I am bound to say, No, I cannot. Whoever says he can, it seems to me, must be taking Berkeley's question in some sophisticated sense. Berkeley has framed his question with some care ; he has chosen his examples, two from the primary qualities, two from the secondary. He is asking the question about *actual* seeing and hearing, and we must not let ourselves be distracted by supplementary questions about possible perception. He is asking it about this A sharp that I am hearing now. Can I conceive it existing unheard ? No ; I cannot ; for if it was unheard it would not be A sharp. He is asking his question about this pink patch I am seeing. Can I conceive it existing unseen ? No ; I cannot ; for if it was unseen it would not be a pink patch. I shall not now go off on the question, What happens to the sound when I cease to hear it, or to the colour in the dark ? The matterist here confines himself to *actual* perception, and so do I. He says that when I actually hear this A sharp, there are two entities, the sensible A sharp in my mind, and the material sound outside. I find that duplication of the object intolerable ; therefore I follow Berkeley and common sense in holding that actual perception is immaterialist. He is not saying that the act of perceiving brings the colour or the sound into existence. Idealists take that view, but they ought not to father their views on Berkeley. He is simply saying that *existence* adds nothing to perception ; for " I hear a sound existing," or " I hear a sound and it exists " are simply long-winded statements, and mean no more than " I hear a sound."

Pass on now to section 23. Here we are in a new chapter of psychology ; we have left sense perception behind, and are dealing with the imagination. Berkeley now voices the difficulty which we all feel about his system at first. If we take complex things, like trees and books, rather than the simple elements of perception, like sights and sounds, it does seem as if we could have an object of sense unperceived. " Surely there's nothing easier than to imagine trees, for instance, in a park, or books existing in a closet, and no body by to perceive them." Quite so, says Berkeley, but that is not sense perception ; that is imagination. Consider your instance with care. What exactly have you done ? You have framed a mental picture of tree or book, and have omitted to include an observer. I should have said, " an observer other than yourself," for *you* are tacitly included in the picture. *You* are observing the book or the tree imagined. *You* are picturing. *You* are imagining ; for there is no imagination without an imaginer ; mental imagery without a mind is nonsense. Your pictured book or tree are not material or absolute ; nor are they imagined as material or absolute ; they are imagined as ordinary books or trees, *i.e.* as perceived or perceivable books or trees, in actual or possible relation to the mind. Imagined existence is imagined perception,[1] not matter ; if you think you are imagining matter, you are mistaken ; you are probably just visualizing a word of six letters beginning with *m* ; you cannot imagine the unimaginable. Your

[1] See the important entries, *PC* 472, 473, and my notes there.

instance proves nothing to the point ; " it only shows you have the power of imagining or forming ideas in your mind ; but it does not show that you can conceive it possible, the objects of your thought may exist without the mind."

The two sections together form a double-barrelled argument against matter ; the right barrel accounts for sensed matter, and the choke barrel accounts for imagined matter. The argument throughout is straightforward and linear ; it is entirely an appeal to empirical, verifiable fact, and contains no *a priori* or transcendental admixture. Berkeley is not arguing that our minds create reality, or determine it, or condition it ; he is not arguing that we impose our forms or categories upon it. He is simply arguing that we cannot apprehend matter either by sense or by imagination. We cannot see, touch, or imagine the " something we know not what."

Part of the difficulty felt about this passage is due to Berkeley's elastic use of the terms *conceive* and *perceive*, and some critics have charged him with cloaking ambiguities of thought under imprecision of language. This charge rests on a misapprehension. Berkeley can be as precise and nice as any lexicographer when he needs to be ; but he would have died long ago if he had spoken with the precision of a dictionary. He has a living thought to express and he must be allowed a living medium. He speaks the vernacular,[1] as we all do, when we are in earnest and in touch with reality. He is thinking aloud, and of course he will not cramp his style with pedantic exactitude. His terms may be elastic, but his readers can easily find their meaning from the context. In these sections *conceive* and *perceive* have to cover a wide

---

[1] Note the "You may so " (§ 23)—a Dublin idiom as vigorous to-day as it was in Berkeley's day.

range of thought-forms, which overlap and coalesce. Sometimes they have specific psychological force ; at other times they are used broadly, as we use *apprehend*, leaving it to the context to determine what form of apprehension is intended. It would be a great mistake to try to pin *conceive* down to higher forms and *perceive* to lower forms ; for it is clear that they both are at times applied to sense, to imagination, and to " pure thought."

CHAPTER IX

EFFECTS AND CAUSES

(*Principles*, §§ 25–29)

IMMATERIALISM without its proper doctrine of effects and causes is an academic exercise of intellect. It does not become a serious business, it cannot translate into terms of living experience, so long as little material causes are included in one's picture of nature or philosophy of the world. The mind may be satisfied that material substance is not wanted ; the man remains unconvinced, until he surrenders those little causes and takes what Berkeley offers in their place. Many have said [1] that they found Berkeley's teaching unanswerable, but unconvincing. That is largely because they divorce his denial of matter from his denial of the material cause.

Berkeley's teaching on cause may be summarized as follows : there are no material or unthinking causes ; the only true causes are spirits or minds ; God is the sole cause of change in nature ; you and I have a derived and limited power of the cause. " Nature " is an ordered system of effects which are not true causes ; in virtue, however, of the order, the regularity, and the uniformity of natural events, one effect serves as a sign of another effect with which it is customarily conjoined. Such signs are popularly known as causes, and are causes in a subsidiary and improper sense of that term. Thus if we

---

[1] Berkeley knew men would say it, and puts the quip into the mouth of Hylas. *Three Dialogues*, ii, *ad fin.* ; *cf.* Hume, *Essays*, vol. ii, Note N, p. 554.

allow ourselves to speak of " natural causes," we must mean merely customary signs.

Sections 25–29 cover Berkeley's theory of causality proper ; here we meet the passivity of all objects of sense, the train of changing events which postulates cause, the activity of the little cause which is I myself, and that of the great Cause who operates the vast system of effects, of which I am aware, but which I know I do not cause. Sections 62–66 contain Berkeley's subsidiary doctrine of natural causation, which we should now call " the regularity view." Causality is touched on in other passages also, *e.g.* in sections 50–51, 102–7, and in section 53, where hints are given as to the sources of Berkeley's doctrine.[1]

Berkeley begins with the effects ;[2] and we must remember that, for him, effects are effects, just as causes are causes. We often think of both rôles as combined in one thing. The mill-wheel, we should say, is effect and cause. Its turning is effected by the water, and causes the grinding of the corn. But that is not so for Berkeley ; a cause, for him, is a real cause, a *causa causans*, an agent ; hence there is no sharing between cause and effect ; an effect, being an effect, cannot be or become an agent. The flow of the water, the turning of the wheel, and the grinding of the corn are thus one continuous

[1] In Malebranche Berkeley found, I believe, the support he needed for his doctrine of cause, if not its source. In *PC* 548 there is an unmistakable reference to Malebranche's famous statement that we do not move our arms, not knowing how to do so. Berkeley may have thought that Malebranche attributed too little to the human spirit, but the two thinkers were at one in ascribing all the works of nature to the immediate operation of God. Berkeley might be called an occasionalist, without the occasion. The " occasion," for him, is matter in disguise (§§ 53, 70*ff.*). He rejects it and the artificial theory of cause which goes with it ; but he fully agrees with the occasionalists in holding the passivity of all objects of sense and in confining true causality to spirit.

[2] Hence I have placed EFFECTS before CAUSES in the chapter heading.

passive process. In that light his opening statement should be read : " All our ideas, sensations, notions, or the things which we perceive, by whatsoever names they may be distinguished, are visibly inactive, there is nothing of power or agency included in them. So that one idea or object of thought cannot produce or make any altera-tion in another." This is a devastating statement, the full force and scope of which dawns on the reader only when he reminds himself that Berkeley's *ideas* are *things*, and that therefore Berkeley is here stating that all sensible things are passive effects, entirely devoid of causal activity of their own, and is asking us, in the teeth of common opinion and inveterate habits of thought and speech, to view the world of sense, in whole and part and particle, as lying " all Danae " [1] to the spirit.

What reason does Berkeley give ? He says that " all our ideas . . . are visibly inactive." " Visibly inactive " is a pregnant phrase, as the context shows ; it does not mean merely that they look inactive, though that is true enough ; it means that, being in the mind, they are fully open to inspection ; we can see into the heart of them ; we can see for ourselves that " there is nothing of power or agency included in them." Locke and the corpuscu-larians attributed mysterious powers and potencies to " every drop of water, every grain of sand " (§ 101) ; but these powers and potencies vanish in the light of the *esse est percipi*, like night when day comes. " Since they and every part of them exist only in the mind, it follows that there is nothing in them but what is perceived." The things I see and touch are all in the light of mind ; they have no secrets ; no part of them is in the dark of matter. I can speak of them and their contents with confidence. I cannot be wrong if I declare what I see,

[1] " Now lies the Earth all Danae to the stars," Tennyson, *The Princess*.

and I see that the things around me are inactive, and have not the power of the cause.

Is this doctrine common sense or the opposite? We scatter the term *cause* freely in its weaker sense, when we mean merely a sign, or symptom, or antecedent, or reason, or ground; we are not so free with it when we have agency in mind, when we are thinking of efficient causality which gets things done and makes changes begin to be. The average man would go a long way with Berkeley here. He might not like to admit that there is *no* activity in the sensible thing; but he probably thinks of nature as being 99 per cent. passive with spots of activity few and far between. He divides the animate world from the inanimate, expecting causality in the former, but not in the latter, expecting agents to act and inanimate things to "stay put." The exceptions, usually admitted, are very big things, the minute parts of things, and very distant things. We think of the distant moon as acting on the sea water and making it ebb and flow, and when we see the buoy at the estuary mouth pointing seawards and suddenly turn with the tide and point landwards, it is hard to rule out activity. Similarly, we think of gravitation as a force emanating from the centre of the earth, and somehow drawing the apple towards it. The minute parts of the magnet " act," we say, on the needle, and the minute parts of almost any external thing we credit with the power of " acting " on our sense organs, or of sending impulses or messages to the brain, and chemical changes, in general, are constantly spoken of as the action of one thing on another.

If we are asked *how* such " causes " act, we must remain silent; we have no notion of activity other than that of animate beings; and when we scrutinize any case of physical causation, the alleged causality oozes out

of it, and becomes regular sequence and ordered movement. The reason seems to be that, as Berkeley teaches,
things are what we see and feel them to be. The sensible
constituents of the sensible thing are throughout perceivable ; we have, or may have, the evidence of our
senses about every part of the sensible. We can go on
subdividing beyond the practical limits of vision, but we
cannot suppose the visible made up of elements by nature
invisible. The sensible thing, thus, in whole and part,
is an immediate object of the mind ; it is, in Berkeley's
terminology, an *idea*, and an idea cannot be, or be like,
an active being. " Whence it plainly follows that extension, figure and motion cannot be the cause of our
sensations. To say, therefore, that these are the effects
of powers resulting from the configuration, number,
motion, size etc. of corpuscles must certainly be false."

Broadly, Berkeley's contention is that nature is an
ordered scene of passive realities moved by an agency not
their own, and is not a collection of animated objects
able to act and cause. The justice of this contention is
seen by putting the alternative. If all, or any, unthinking
things were true causes, able to make changes begin to
be, as we do when we push or pull or plan or purpose, the
uniformity of nature would go up in smoke ; the multitude
of agents would spell chaos ; anarchy would replace the
reign of law ; multicausality yields multiformity, and the
uniformity we find implies the *una vera causa*, the one true
Cause. Could the work of science go on, could the
ordinary business of life go on, if the sensible things around
us were true agents or causing causes ? Wind, stream, fire,
tide, gravity, magnetism, electricity, and all the other
" forces of nature " are, it would seem, adequately
explained as the co-ordinated movement of passive things,
completely devoid of spontaneity. If the passive appears

active, it is because at sight or sound of the phenomena we make incipient movements in ourselves which we wrongly ascribe to them. This sympathy with nature, or rather *empathy*, goes far to explain the causal efficacy attributed to some unthinking things. As we sway our bodies to the desired path of the billiard ball, or drum with our fingers or our feet, so we move to the rhythm of the wind or to the flow of the water. When we try to picture what actually makes the apple fall, we imagine ourselves reaching up and pulling it down ; and when in real earnest, poetry apart, we attribute causal power to wind or wave or centre of the earth, we are projecting into passive things the causal impulses which stir in us.

Cause has a place of honour in the Berkeleian system. Berkeley denies causal power to unthinking things in order to place it where it properly belongs ; he wants to end that indiscriminate use of the word *cause* which takes the heart out of it and explains nothing. Strongly he insists that unthinking things are not causes ; equally strongly he insists that they are effects ; they are without spontaneity, without principle of action or power of self-movement, but they are not outside the causal relation ; a cause they must have ; their passivity is a foil for the activity of spirit ; it is the anvil for the hammer of the act of God and the act of man.

Berkeley's account of the causality of spirit consists of a broad statement of the need for a cause, an explanation of what he means by spirit, a description of the causality we feel within, and an inference to causality without.

He starts from daily experience. " We perceive a continual succession of ideas." That is, we perceive a succession of events, a succession of idea-things, a succession of significant things. Things come and go before our eyes. There must be some cause of this coming and going ; at times we can take it all for granted, but in our speculative moments, when, for instance, we are watching the break of day, or an eclipse, we readily endorse the words, " There is therefore some cause of these ideas whereon they depend, and which produces and changes them." The ideas, whether singly or in combination, are not the cause ; for they are passive ; material substance has been shown to be impossible ; we must therefore postulate as cause " an incorporeal, active substance or spirit."

The notion of spirit, lightly touched in sections 2 and 7, is then discussed. Spirit, for Berkeley, is substance, agency, and cause, a positive dynamic, not a negative conception ; it is more than spiritual atmosphere or tendency ; he accepts, of course, the things of spirit, such as virtue, wisdom, and justice, and is willing to call them spirit ; he recognizes spiritual achievement and environment, and what might be called the ether of spirit ; but such ether radiates from radiant points. Berkeleian spirit is, first and foremost, *a* spirit, a focus, a unity, a centre of active experience, defined as " one simple, undivided, active being." These terms are chosen to contrast with sense. Sensible things are many and complex ; spirit is one and simple. Sensible things are divisible, spirit not. Sensible things are passive, spirit is active. The activity of spirit takes two forms ; it perceives ideas and produces ideas, or operates about them ; hence spirit is both understanding and will.

The " idea of spirit " now comes under fire. This looks to us like an academic question about words, but we can understand why Berkeley returns to it again and again,[1] and attaches such importance to it, if we bear in mind what has been said about idea as passive effect and spirit

---

[1] See especially §§ 135*ff.*, and below, p. 147 ; *cf. PC* 490.

as active cause. His whole conception of spirit as cause is at stake ; for if you could have an idea of God or the soul, then spirit and sensible thing, active cause and passive effect, are confounded. Spirit and idea differ in kind ; and if you could have an idea of spirit, you would have a passive picture of that which acts—which is impossible. Pictures or likenesses of spirit are as impossible as pictures or likenesses of matter. We can try for ourselves ; we know spirit by the effects of its activities, but not by any passive representation. We know our active powers, will and understanding, from within, in their exercise ; but we have no mental picture of them, nor of a substance supporting them.

The denial of an idea of spirit has its dangers, and Berkeley was alive to those dangers and deals with them in sections 135 *ff.*, where he is concerned with self-know-ledge. Some people would argue that if there is no idea of spirit, then we cannot know the existence of God and the soul. Berkeley wants to avoid giving that handle to scepticism, and at the same time to preserve intact his sharp distinctions between active and passive, cause and effect, spirit and idea. It is a delicate issue, because the term *idea* has so many varieties of meaning in ordinary speech. In the first edition Berkeley concedes (§ 140) that " in a large sense, indeed, we may be said to have an idea of *spirit*, that is we understand the meaning of the word. . . ." He thus shows that he is not attacking innocent forms of speech, which simply assert knowledge of spiritual reality ; he is attacking representative ideas of spirit, which make the mind of man the measure of the truth of God ; he is attacking the Lockian concept of the soul and God. He insists that we really know ourselves and know God and finite spirits, but have no pictorial sketch or copy of the essential activity of spirit.

In the second edition Berkeley takes other means to the same end. He introduces the term *notion* to describe the spiritual object of knowledge as an alternative to *idea* " in a large sense." The net result is just the same, and there is no alteration in doctrine involved.[1] The *notion* which Berkeley permits is no cognitive medium, but a linguistic convenience. If a critic says to him, You are a sceptic or agnostic ; you deny that we have an idea of God and the soul, Berkeley replies, No ; I am no sceptic or agnostic. I have a notion of God and the soul, an assured and intelligent knowledge of both.

Having thus set the scene Berkeley proceeds (§§ 28–29) to bring the actors on the stage. He has established the fact of change, the need for cause, and the notion of spirit. Now he produces proof of the causal activity of spirit, human and divine. He does so without any flourish of trumpets ; he does not even raise his voice. He states the facts in simple language, as a man does who is sure of himself. He gives a reason for holding that I cause, and a reason for holding that God causes, and by contrasting the two causes he makes the derived causality of the finite mind a stepping-stone to the creative causality of the infinite Mind. In effect, he argues thus : I know what I can do ; I know what I cannot do. Therefore I know what God can do and does.

The faculty of the imagination furnishes Berkeley's proof of finite causality. In the fact that we imagine, we

---

[1] This second edition alteration appears in §§ 27, 89, 140, 142 ; see also the omission of *notion* in §§ 25, 138. We must not attach an exaggerated importance to this group of changes. Berkeley himself calls it (§ 142) " an affair of verbal concern." The change of term represents no change in teaching whatsoever. Berkeley is simply guarding his doctrine of spirit from a natural misunderstanding ; there is not a shadow of difference between the two editions on the substantial issue. See my " The Alleged Development of Berkeley's Philosophy," *Mind*, lii, N.S. No. 206, pp. 146–47.

first [1] see our active selves as in a mirror ; in inward action we *first* see ourselves as we are. " I find I can excite ideas in my mind at pleasure, and vary and shift the scene as oft as I think fit. 'Tis no more than willing, and straightway this or that idea arises in my fancy : and by the same power it is obliterated, and makes way for another. This making and unmaking of ideas doth very properly denominate the mind active." That is graphic writing, and the psychology is studied from the life. Berkeley does not say *how* the imagination works ; it is not his business to do so ; neither he nor anyone else can do so ; " the remaining-over " of the percept is as great a mystery to-day as when Aristotle coined the phrase. But the fact is there as large as life. I can, within limits, make myself see in the imagination to-day what I saw in the flesh yesterday. I cannot tell how it is done, but I know it is done in accordance with the laws of per-ception and the laws of nature ; it is done *non sine numine Dei* ; but I do it, or help to do it. I imagine ; therefore I act. I act ; therefore I cause.

Now for the contrast. With my activity in fancying compare my passivity in sensing ; with my few little brief idea-images compare the vast system of idea-things ; my imaginings are active ; my sense perception is in large measure reception. Ideas of the imagination prove my activity, for I am their cause, and I know it ; ideas of sense prove the activity of God ; for I am not their cause, and He is. For " when in broad daylight I open my eyes, 'tis not in my power to chuse whether I shall see or no, or to determine what particular objects shall present themselves to my view ; and so likewise as to the hearing and other senses, the ideas imprinted on them

[1] Berkeley accepts, of course, the outward action of finite spirits ; *e.g.* " We move our Legs our selves," *PC* 548 ; *cf. Princ.* 147.

are not creatures of my will. There is therefore some other will or spirit that produces them."

The reader should pause on these words. They have an air of naïveté, almost nonchalance, and the illustration is homely, almost simple-minded. It is easy to be misled by the brevity and restraint of the passage, and to miss its depth and truth.[1] The restraint, as in section 6, is intentional. This is the " direct & brief demonstration " forecast in his *Commentaries*,[2] and a briefer or more direct proof of God's existence has rarely, if ever, appeared in print. The illustration is full of meaning for those familiar with Locke's *Essay*, and Berkeley's first readers must have seen in it a reference to the passage [3] where Locke writes, " But if I turn my eyes at noon towards the sun, I cannot avoid the ideas which the light or sun then produces in me." The two thinkers have performed the same simple experiment in vision, and there is a world of difference in their results. Locke infers " the brisk acting of some objects without me " ; Berkeley infers the act of God.

" There is therefore some other will or spirit that produces them." The words have the eloquence of sincerity. It is the utterance, not of an official tied to a system, but of a free, independent thinker facing the facts of life.[4] Outwardly it is a drab and colourless statement ; but it has overtones. It is a personal, mind-thrilled *credo*, straight from the heart of the cosmos, with the fresh charm of a young man's first articulation of reasoned faith in God. It is often called Berkeley's *causal argument* for the existence of God, and so it is ; but

[1] See above, p. 68–69.
[2] No. 41 ; *cf.* also No. 499, where there are echoes of this passage.
[3] IV xi 5.
[4] Berkeley was in Orders when the *Principles* appeared, but he had thought out this argument long before. I am far from thinking that a theological system is *necessarily* incompatible with freedom of thought.

there is more to it than that.   It is rather an argument *from* God than an argument *to* God.   It is the final outcome of his reading of the perceptual situation.   It is an argument for immaterialism based on the passivity of the sensible object and the implied activity of spirit.   The argument has no sting or grip as long as we attribute causal efficacy to the things we see and touch ; but look around for an active unthinking thing ; hunt for an object of sense with causal powers ; and when you are satisfied that there are none such, *then* come back and read section 29 again ; it takes on a new aspect.

CHAPTER X

THE REAL AND THE IMAGINARY

(*Principles*, §§ 30–33)

BERKELEY's use of the term *idea* to describe the object of sense leaves him open to the charge of having no criterion of reality. Those who would rather mock than understand him usually take this line. They pretend that he is using *idea* in the colloquial sense. A superior smile forms on their lips as they say, " Ha ! ha ! Heat and the idea of heat are all one to him ; the good bishop doesn't know the difference between putting his hand into the fire and dreaming that he has done so."

Matter, on the other hand, is supposed to supply the required criterion. Macbeth in doubt asks, " Is this a dagger which I see before me ? " ; we take it that he is asking whether it is a material dagger or " a dagger of the mind." No one has ever explained *how* matter would help Macbeth, on the stage or off ; but the legend persists that *somehow* a real dagger would boil down to matter, and an imaginary dagger to nothing at all. In consequence timid folk hang on to material substance as to a lifeline.

In sections 30–33 Berkeley shows that his immaterialism in no way confounds the real and the imaginary ; he lays down clear-cut psychological distinctions which are those we use in ordinary life, and he advances that ultimate criterion which is to most people the final court of appeal in times of stress. When a man is seriously in doubt, when fact and fancy seem confounded, and " nothing is but what is not," he does not turn to this unknown abstraction, matter ; he turns to the concrete, to the known and the familiar, to nature and nature's God. Berkeley furnishes the philosophical ground of this instinct, and tells us that reality is what God made, and appearance what man imagines.

"The ideas imprinted on the senses by the Author of nature are called *real things*, and those excited in the imagination being less regular, vivid, and constant, are more properly termed *ideas*, or *images of things*, which they copy and represent." The contrast between the two types of ideas is the basis of Berkeley's account of reality ; and Macbeth's question would become, in Berkeley's technique, Is this an idea of sense or an idea of the imagination ? Or, in other words, Am I really seeing, or only imagining ? If it is an idea of sense, if I am really seeing, then God gives it me, and it is real. If it is not an idea of sense, then God has not given it to me. I am not really seeing it ; I make it. I imagine it ; it is an image of a thing.

The term "Author of nature" should be noted. It does not quite satisfy our sense of reality to be told that God made our object ; we demand to know also whether or not it is part of nature. Berkeley accepts that demand ; he lays great stress on nature in this passage. He does not bring back matter disguised as nature, of course ; "nature" does not stand for any non-spiritual agency. "Nature" is a general name for the works of God, which adds an important hint as to the manner of God's working and the character of His works. Our ideas of sense are the works of God, and not copies of them, but to say that and stop there might give the impression that the Berkeleian world of sense was a haphazard, disjointed, lawless affair like a train of fancies. When we are told that God imprints ideas upon our minds, we can hardly help thinking of the occasional, intermittent action of a man ; the notion of nature is the needed corrective ; for God imprints ideas which form nature, which are nature, and therefore His action is continuous, uniform, and neverfailing ; His action is action in depth, and we must not think of it as a passing, superficial impression on the mind. Berkeley's ideas of sense are idea-things, ideas that *are* things, not ideas *of* things.[1] Therefore when he says that God imprints ideas of sense on our minds, he is simply considering that aspect of creation which concerns human perception ; the phrase *implies* that God's continuous creative action makes and sustains a vast system of significant things and exhibits them to us, and in them, as in a printed page, we read God's standing orders and messages, thus learning what we should do and what we should think. Nature, the sum total of these significant entities, is far too vast for any finite mind to grasp. Our feeling for nature, voiced in the demand for reality, is an appeal from the partial datum to the total ; it is a feeling for wholeness and system in the works of God. This does not mean that a man must be in a religious frame of mind to know the difference between fact and fancy ; but it does mean that a full *rationale* of our belief in reality is impossible without an intelligent belief in God.

Berkeley's philosophy of nature is an education of the religious sense. He is teaching about God in teaching about nature. We learn of God in His works, which not only prove Him, but praise Him. Nature's God, seen as Berkeley sees Him, can be no aggregate, nor tendency, nor force, nor mere mover, but a rational intelligent being, benevolent and wise. For " the ideas of sense . . . are not excited at random, as those which are the effects of human wills often are, but in a regular train or series,

[1] " Of & thing causes of mistake," *PC* 115, where see my note.

the admirable connexion whereof sufficiently testifies the wisdom and benevolence of its author. Now the set rules or established methods, wherein the mind we depend on excites in us the ideas of sense, are called the *laws of nature*."

Thus the Berkeleian ideas of sense, which look so casual and wayward at first, have been drawn into a universal scheme or system, governed by God-given laws, sharply contrasted with mental imagery and the work of fancy which are not governed by those laws. Sensible reality is nature and her laws, a regular, orderly, and connected system of sense data. A knowledge of nature is a knowledge of the laws of nature, *i.e.* a knowledge of the " consistent, uniform working " of its Author. Thanks to our knowledge of these laws we are not at the mercy of events ; we can foretell the future by reading it in the present. We can predict the sunrise, because the long dark of night is uniformly followed by day. We know in advance that wood will burn, and water not, and knowing such uniformities we can live ordered and useful lives.

Berkeley then notices two common misreadings of our sentient experience. We read effects as causes, and customary connections as necessary connections. We misinterpret the uniformity and regularity of nature. We confuse sequence with agency ; observing that A is regularly followed by B, we conclude that A is the cause of B. Again the connections are so often repeated that we take them to be necessary ; we suppose that B *must* follow A. But there is no *must* in the case. The connections might have been otherwise. Though regular, they are not rigid ; though customary, they may be changed. The cast-iron sequences postulated by mechanism are not found in nature. Law is founded on will, not on necessity. Therefore there is room in God's world for the supernatural, for the exception to the rule, and for miracle.[1]

The contrast between the vagaries of human fancy and the uniformity and regularity of God's works must now be examined on its psychological side. How do we know the difference between real and imaginary in actual life ? What are the psychological distinctions between ideas of sense and those of the imagination ? Berkeley has studied the question carefully. The contrast is firmly fixed in his philosophy and fully explained by it.

The contrast is, of course, on a background of resemblance ; ideas of sense and ideas of the imagination have something in common, or there would be little point in contrasting them. They are alike, and therefore Berkeley can call them both *ideas* ; they agree, and that is why their differences are so important. The real dagger and the "dagger in the mind," though poles apart, are tragically alike. Now, for Berkeley, both daggers are " in the mind " ; both are ideas, for both are immediate objects of their respective faculties. *Idea*, when Berkeley wrote, was the term in vogue ; it was broad enough to cover objects of both faculties, and Berkeley had to use it in spite of its disadvantages.[2] In this very passage he shows himself well aware of the narrower usage ; he grants that ideas of the imagination " are more properly termed *ideas*," but he held, quite rightly, that some term had to be found to express the basic resemblance of the two different objects. Hume felt the difficulty ; modern psychology feels it ; and Berkeley's solution was, in its day, as good as any. Impressions and ideas, sensations and images, sense data and *imaginata*, are all equally *perceived*.

---

[1] *cf.* §§ 62, 106-7, 146, 151 ; *PC* 734.
[2] See below, pp. 116-18.

Sense and imagination use the same cerebral tracts and mechanisms ; the outer eye and the inner eye are physiologically connected ; what I see to-day I shall dream of to-night and visualize to-morrow ; and therefore in using the one official label *idea* for the common features of the two object types, Berkeley is simply recognizing fact, and is doing nothing to weaken the distinction between real and imaginary. No trained philosopher, at any rate, should charge him with doing so.

Turn now to the distinctions, metaphysical and psychological, which Berkeley draws. I will set them forth in tabular form.

IDEAS OF SENSE	IDEAS OF THE IMAGINATION
(Metaphysical)	
imprinted by God	the creatures of the mind
less dependent on the spirit which perceives them	of its own framing
excited by the will of a more powerful spirit	
real things (more real)	images of things which they copy and represent
(Psychological)	
stronger	fainter
more lively	less lively, less vivid
more distinct	less distinct
steady	less constant
orderly, coherent	often excited at random
in a regular train or series	less regular

The psychology here is a careful piece of introspection, faithfully and guardedly expressed. Hume echoes several of the distinctions. The metaphysical distinctions are, to the immaterialist, inevitable deductions from the psychological facts.

A preliminary remark on the table is required. Berkeley makes the clean cut between the God-given object and the man-made object; but he does not mean us to infer that God has nothing to do with our imaginings, or that we have nothing to do with our own sentience. We could not imagine without the divine aid; our imagination is an instrument we use, but do not make and scarcely understand. In sentience, of course, we bear our part. *We* sense; *we* see, and unless we open our eyes and fix our gaze, we shall not see; but we do not make what we see, and we do go far to make what we imagine. We do not originate what we sense, and we do originate, in great measure, what we imagine.

This distinction is much more intelligible than any distinction which invokes matter. When I am told that the real originates in matter, and the imaginary in mind, I have a glib formula, but am no wiser. But when I am told that God gives me to see the dawn of day, and gives me the dawn to see, I do understand, in a measure, what has been said, for it fits in with the rest of my experience; and when I draw my curtains and see the crimson and the gold in the eastern sky, I say sincerely, " It's grand, thank God." But tell me those colours originate in material substance, originate in " something we know not what "—you might as well tell me they originate in mumbo-jumbo.

Consider now *seriatim* Berkeley's main psychological distinctions between the sensible and the imaginary. *Strong* and *faint*, as applied to objects, are readily understood. Strong objects stand out against their background; they are startling, forceful, truculent. Like Hume's impressions, " they strike upon the mind " with force and liveliness. The sight of a cricket match on a sunny day is *strong*; the grass is verdant green; the crease and the flannels white as snow; the batsman can see the seam on the brown ball; the thud of the stroke resounds. But afterwards, when you lean back in your armchair and hold a mental *post-mortem* on your "duck," your visualizing is a very pale edition of your seeing; bowler and batsman are shadowy forms; sounds are dim; lines are faint; colours have gone like a faded photograph.

Distinctness is an important trait. The idea of sense is distinct; the image is blurred. The percept is sharply defined; there is no confusing it with other things. Images are dim and dull and shade off into other things. Stooks of corn in the moonlit harvest field are beautiful, but difficult to handle; things are not distinct "*incerto sub lumine lunae*." The imagination is, relatively, a moonlit mind, and as the sunlight is to the moonlight, so is the idea of sense to its reproduction in image or memory.

The idea of sense is steady; the image inconstant; the percept is fixed or relatively so, and if our object, say a dagger, keeps flickering in and out, we put it down as unreal at once. Of course the object may disappear regularly and return regularly, like the flash of a revolving lighthouse; in such a case the inconstancy has merged in a higher constancy, and the object takes its place in an orderly pattern of space-time events.

Berkeley states most of these criteria in relative terms, and few, if any, absolutely. The facts dictate that course. Broadly, percepts are strong, and images weak; but you may meet many a weak percept and strong image. Some portrait painters have such strong images that, it is said, they can paint from them. At dusk or dawn ideas of sense may lack distinctness, and under stress and strain images will attain uncanny definition. In both types of object many shades, degrees, and modes of steadiness, order, and coherence are to be found. In consequence, one subjective criterion of reality is not enough to cover all the cases. In ninety-nine cases out of a hundred the normal person can tell reality at a glance ; the " strength " of the object tells him ; but there will always be the doubtful cases, most of them pathological, and then we must use the other tests that are appropriate.

Even the term *reality* is used by Berkeley in a comparative sense. Ideas, for him, can be more real or less real ; it does not follow that he would accept the idealist doctrine of degrees of reality. We must remember that in this passage he is speaking only of sensible reality. There are spiritual realities for him, and he certainly could not accept a doctrine of degrees of reality if it blurred the distinction between the infinite spirit and the finite. For practical purposes the God-given character of sensible things is an absolute criterion, and on that ground they " are called real things." A few lines down Berkeley says they " are allow'd to have more reality in them." There he may be speaking " off book," and merely echoing Descartes, or, as I prefer to think, he may have his eye on those elements in the true imagination which cannot be excluded altogether from God's real world.

Berkeley has thus built up a reasonable account of sensible reality, and has set it over against the cloud-capped towers of the imagination ; he has done so without the slightest help from matter. He has drawn true, important, and verifiable distinctions between the real and the imaginary ; he has sufficiently distinguished the two types of object both in regard to their origin and their appearance, and he has held them both within the scope of the *esse est percipi.* Berkeley has thus shown that the immaterialist has as strong a sense of reality and as good criteria of reality as any one else, and that to surrender material substance is not to surrender reality, nor to part company with sanity or efficiency. He showed the same by his life. A saner man than he never stepped. He moved through this life to the next with confident serenity. He had no haunting doubts about his senses. Assured that the good God who gave him his senses gave him also objects of sense, he simply took the given as given. He had no illusions ; his imagination was his servant, not his master ; he handled with ease and grace and " natural piety " the data which form the order of nature.

CHAPTER XI

CROSS-EXAMINATION

THIRTEEN OBJECTIONS AND BERKELEY'S REPLIES

(Principles, §§ 34–84)

BERKELEY has anticipated almost every possible objection to his system. His keen dramatic sense, evidenced in his *Dialogues*, has enabled him to enter into the minds of readers and critics, and to see his own views as others see them. A professor of theology used to open his course of lectures with the words, " Gentlemen, you cannot invent a new heresy." One might almost say of the *Principles*, " You cannot invent a new objection." Certainly the thirteen objections, advanced and answered in these fifty-one sections, form a comprehensive list. Few of them are " period " objections ; most of them would occur to any thinker in any age who tried to dispense with matter.

Berkeley's answers form a fine piece of controversial writing. That in youth he should have been able to see his own views so clearly from other viewpoints is a tribute to his detachment, his sincerity, and his speculative powers. He has stated each objection frankly, and he claims (§ 85) to have given each its full force. His answers are expressed in simple language, and nowhere, with the possible exception of the fourth objection,[1] does he show any trace of reserve or hesitation. He appears as a complete master of immaterialism ; he moves easily in all its details ; he knows what others will urge ; he knows

---

[1] See below, p. 120*ff*.

what he wants to say in reply, and he says it clearly
and forcibly.

Whether readers to-day should spend much time on
this part of the work, themselves must judge. These
sections do not contribute much to the positive exposition
of immaterialism ; they were not intended to so ; but
they are not barren controversy. They contribute to an
appreciation of the system. The founder of immaterialism
here steps, as it were, into the witness-box, and submits
to cross-examination on his views, and his answers help
to set the points at issue in a clear light. The first five
objections (§§ 34-49) are the most important, and they
receive special attention here.

TABLE OF THE OBJECTIONS [1]

IMMATERIALISM

I	Reduces nature to an illusion (§§ 34-40)
II	Confounds real and imaginary (§ 41)
III	Conflicts with our sense of externality (§§ 42-44)
IV	Must suppose the intermittent existence of the objects of sense, their annihilation, and perpetual re-creation (§§ 45-48)
V	Makes mind extended and shaped (§§ 49)
VI	Undermines the principles of science (§ 50)
VII	Substitutes spiritual causes for material (§§ 51-53)
⎰VIII	Is in opposition to general consent and cannot ex-
⎱ IX	plain the prevalence of the belief in matter (§§ 54-57)
X	Is incompatible with mathematical and scientific truth (§§ 58-59)

[1] The numbering given here is Berkeley's, except that he has omitted
to number the ninth, which opens out of his answer to the eighth, and the
thirteenth, which looks like an afterthought. Fraser (vol. i, 1901, pp.
227-31) counts them as fourteen, and Jessop as sixteen (Analysis prefixed
to his edition). These differences arise because the digressions which
obscure the twelfth may rank as separate objections, or, as in my numbering,
as varieties of the one main objection.

XI   Cannot explain the mechanisms of organic life
      (§§ 60–66)
XII   Has not refuted other conceptions of matter, *viz*. the
      occasion without sensible qualities (§§ 67–76), the
      occasion without qualities known by our present
      senses (§§ 77–78), the occasion as a completely un-
      known entity (§ 79), indefinite existence (§§ 80–81)
XIII Contradicts Holy Scripture (§§ 82–84)

To go through all these objections in detail would
involve much repetition of previous argument.   Instead
I will state in Berkeley's words the pith of each objection,
combining those which are virtually identical, and will
summarize his answers.

Objections I and II (§§ 34–41)

" All that is real and substantial in nature is
banished out of the world ;   and instead
thereof a chimerical scheme of ideas takes
place.   All things that exist, exist only in the
mind, that is, they are purely notional.   What
therefore becomes of the sun, moon, and stars ?
What must we think of houses, rivers, mountains, trees, stones ;   nay, even of our own
bodies ?   Are all these but so many chimeras
and illusions on the fancy ? "

Berkeley, in reply, can only repeat what he has said
clearly before, *viz*. that his denial of material substance
detracts in no way from reality, that nature and the
objects of sense remain intact, and that by calling them
ideas and making them exist only in the mind, he does
not make them " notional " (*i.e.* subjective), nor confound
them with objects of the imagination.   He adds an abstract

of his teaching (§ 36), and a strong reassertion of his belief in the senses (§ 40).

In weighing this reply the reader should bear in mind the two points, which are the pivots of correct Berkeleian exegesis : (1) Berkeley is using the term *substance* technically ; he is not denying the existence of what are popularly called substances, such as the sun, moon, stars, etc. ; on the contrary he is whole-heartedly affirming their existence and explaining it. The only substance he is denying is " material substance "—an unknown and unknowable, non-spiritual support of things, the product of philosophers' inventiveness. (2) " Existence in the mind " is not mental existence, but existence for the mind, existence in relation to the mind, as opposed to the " absolute existence " or existence without any relation to the mind claimed for matter by its champions. When these two distinctions are borne in mind, objections of this type are seen to be shallow, flimsy, and unfair.

But there is a supplementary objection of greater weight ; it is dealt with in section 39, where Berkeley gives, for the first time, an important and interesting explanation of his peculiar terminology. We may put it this way : if Berkeley has fairly met the main objection, if he is genuine in saying, " That the things I see with my eyes and touch with my hands do exist, really exist, I make not the least question," then his position is not far from that of common sense. Why then does he not speak the language of common sense ? Let him drop these shocking paradoxes. Let him call a spade a spade, a thing a thing, and an idea an idea. Why should he try to persuade us that " we eat and drink ideas, and are clothed with ideas " ?

Berkeley replies with an apology and an explanation. He admits that his technical term *idea* sounds harsh in an everyday context ; but he pleads that we ought not to mind the sound of the words, provided they express the truth ; and it is true, he says, that we eat, drink, and wear " the immediate objects of sense which cannot exist unperceived or without the mind."

What name, then, should the philosopher give to the immediate object ? Each generation will answer that question in its own way. If Berkeley were writing to-day he would use the term now in vogue, namely, *sense datum* ; but in his day it was a choice between *idea* and *thing*. On reflection [1] he decided for *idea* in spite of its drawbacks. For two reasons *thing* would not do ; (1) *thing* is commonly supposed to mean a material thing, " somewhat existing, without the mind,"[2] (2) *thing* has too wide a denotation ; for it is often applied by philosophers to the active being, the *res cogitans*, the thinking thing. If it sounds ridiculous to say we eat and drink ideas, it also sounds ridiculous, indeed it *is* ridiculous, to say we eat and drink things, where *things* is taken to mean either material substance or thinking things. *Idea*, on the other hand, expressed relatedness to mind, immediacy, and passivity, and therefore at the time it served Berkeley's turn very well.

Berkeley was no pedant ; he wrote living language ; he wished to be understood, and when nothing turns on it, he is perfectly willing to call objects of sense *things*, and he often does so. Indeed, he often speaks of visible,

---

[1] He considered the question carefully ; see *PC* 644 and my note on 369.

[2] This supposition is by no means universal or well founded, as a glance at the dictionary shows (*sub* " thing "). Many of its typical usages imply relation to the mind, and perhaps it originally meant a minded object, an object of attention. The etymology of the word is not certain. " thing " may be connected with *denken* ; but the authorities prefer to derive it from *tempus*. A very early meaning of *thing* is *meeting*. Some think that the Latin *res* is derived from *reor*. In Hebrew the one word *deber* does duty for thing, word, and business.

tangible, and sensible ideas, treating *idea* and *thing* as equivalents. He moved with the times, however, and later in life when the term *idea* no longer suited, he modified his technique without any alteration of doctrine. In his *Alciphron* very largely, and in his *Siris* almost completely, he gave up calling the object of sense *idea*, and adopted *appearance* (the Latin for the Greek) in its place.

Objection III (§§ 42-44)

" We see things actually without or at a distance
   from us, and which consequently do not exist in
   the mind."

Berkeley in reply touches on the dream argument, but he does not press it. He says that we often dream we see things at a distance which are not at a distance. But he was not satisfied with that answer, which brings the real world too close to the world of dreams. Accordingly he takes us from dream to vision itself, and says that if the true theory of vision were adopted, as put forth in his *Essay Towards a New Theory of Vision*, then we should not say when speaking precisely that we see things at a distance, but that we see objects in our minds which suggest things outside.

In considering this reply, we must remember that the metaphysics of the *Essay on Vision* is not that of the *Principles*. The two works were on the stocks together, but in the earlier publication Berkeley disclosed only one-half, so to speak, of his immaterialism ; he took ideas of sight into the mind, but maintained that ideas of touch were of a different genus, and allowed his readers to assume that they (the ideas of touch) were outside the mind in matter. In consequence a good deal of the metaphysics of the earlier publication was of an *ad interim* character, and is virtually superseded by that of the *Principles*. Berkeley published a *Vindication* of his *Essay on Vision* and never withdrew it ; none the less he virtually admits the truth of what I have just said by his reference here, " even in that treatise."

The question of distance is directly affected by this change of standpoint. It is one thing to say we do not *see* distance, when you have a tangible world and tangible distance in the background ; it is another thing to give that answer when you have gone the whole way and admitted the tangible world into the mind on the same footing as the visible world. I think, therefore, that the statements about distance in section 44, though they are in strict conformity with the half-way position of the *Essay on Vision*, are not explicit enough for a reader of the *Principles*. The immaterialist is not required to hold that there is no external world, and that he sees everything, light, colours, forms, and figures, in the flat, right up against his eye and virtually part of his body ; and if this passage is made to prove it, it is made to prove too much.[1]

Visible and tangible distance, sensible environment, outness from the body—these things are quite compatible with Berkeley's immaterialism, and in that sense Berkeley accepts the externality of the world.[2] He rejects the absolute distance of the Newtonian physics, and an external *material* world outside the range of mind. But he does not deny distance *in toto* in the *Principles*. Indeed,

[1] The parallel problem of the heterogeneity of the visible and the tangible undergoes a similar change. In the *Essay on Vision* visible and tangible are heterogeneous because the former is in the mind, the latter not. In the *Principles* they both are in the mind, but Berkeley can still call them heterogeneous, because they are data of different senses.

[2] In § 90 he applies the term *external* to things.

he repeatedly recognizes relative distance (§§ 58, 112–13), and his case for relative motion rests altogether upon the supposition of " two bodies, whereof the distance or position in regard to each other is varied." [1]

Berkeley is answering an objector who assumes that things seen at a distance are *eo ipso* outside the mind. Very naturally and properly he appeals to his *Essay on Vision* in order to show the objector that there is much more in the notion of distance than is usually assumed ; but we are not to infer that he reverts to the standpoint of that *Essay*, or that he endorses all that he had previously said on distance. What he does, in effect, is to assume tacitly the objector's antecedent, but to deny his consequent. He assumes that we see things at a distance from us, but he denies that they are outside the mind ; he accepts sensible or perceived distance, but denies material or absolute distance.

Objection IV (§§ 45–48)

" The objects of sense exist only when they are perceived : the trees therefore are in the garden, or the chairs in the parlour, no longer than while there is somebody by to perceive them. Upon shutting my eyes all the furniture in the room is reduced to nothing, and barely upon opening 'em, it is again created."

This objection draws from Berkeley one of his few explicit statements, a decisive statement, on the all-important question of the perceivable. The passage needs careful study, and sections 45 and 48 should be read

---

[1] § 112; see also § 116 where relative space is affirmed, perceived by sense, and related to bodies. Relative space involves relative distance, *i.e.* perceived distance.

continuously at first, for they give the thread of the argument, and sections 46–47 are, as the opening of section 48 shows, a digression. The words quoted above are so forcible and graphic that hasty readers may take them to represent Berkeley's own views. They are the words of the objector, but Berkeley does not at first explicitly dissociate himself from them—a fact which contributes to the difficulty of the passage and is one of the reasons why Berkeley's doctrine of the perceivable has been persistently misrepresented.

The objector urges that the New Principle, *esse est percipi*, carries with it the " in and out " existence of the objects of sense, because it makes their existence depend on the vagaries of my attention. There they are in front of me ; the next moment they are gone to nothing ; then back they come again ; they have been re-created. This objection is no mere extravagance of thought, and Berkeley is right to deal tenderly with it. Many careful thinkers, scientists among them, do hold that colours, sounds, tastes, etc., do actually pass in and out of existence, that they are momentary existences, generated by the sense organ, which appear *de nihilo*, and pass away. The matterist can fall back on matter. He points to it as the permanent behind these transient appearances. The immaterialist, not having this resource, must either accept intermittency and the doctrines which go with it, annihilation and perpetual re-creation, or he must give a new account.

Berkeley does not accept intermittency, and he gives a new account. His reply on the main issue is delayed, but definite, " It does not therefore follow from the foregoing principles, that bodies are annihilated and created every moment, or exist not at all during the intervals between our perception of them." Nothing could be

more explicit.   Whoever, therefore, would make intermittency and the companion doctrines a necessary part
of Berkeley's philosophy, or so interprets that philosophy
that those consequences follow from it, has misunderstood it and is misrepresenting it on a vital particular.[1]

Now consider the text in some detail.   In section 45
Berkeley states the charge brought against him, and without pleading Guilty or Not Guilty he refers the reader
to what he has written in sections 3, 4, etc., and begs
him to consider well " whether he means anything, by
the actual existence of an idea, distinct from its being
perceived."   He specifies " actual existence," for in
effect he is saying to the objector, Whatever be my
answer to your objection, let this be understood at the
outset.   I am meeting you in terms of my New Principle,
esse est percipi.   I take my stand on the nature and meaning
of *existence*.   If you champion the unperceived existence
of what I *actually* see and touch, you are standing up for
a phrase without a meaning.   You lay " absurdities " to
my charge, but you are asking me to assent to meaningless propositions.

[1] Why does Berkeley delay this answer and appear to hesitate about it ?
I suggest the following answer. He had long and carefully considered the
problem (see on § 3 above, pp. 63-64, and *PC* 52 with my note *ib*) and was
sure of his ground. His doctrine of the perceivable is clear and consistent, but none the less the question, Does the perceivable exist ? places
him in a tactical difficulty. Had he replied bluntly, Yes, the casual reader
might think that he was eating his words, granting existence to things
unperceived, and bringing matter back in the guise of the perceivable.
If, on the other hand, he had said, No, the perceivable does not exist,
he would be giving a totally false impression of his teaching, and the reader
would take him to mean that sensible reality was a passing show without
permanence or substance and confined to that handful of objects we happen
to be perceiving at the moment. Does the perceivable *exist* ? By delaying
his answer a little, Berkeley forces the objector to meditate on his own
question, and consider the meaning of " exist." For until he has done so,
until he has grasped Berkeley's conception of existence, he could not
understand Berkeley's conception of the perceivable.

Pass on now to sections 46 and 47. These are, as I have said, a digression, in that they delay Berkeley's final answer to the objection ; but they are a very relevant digression. The difficulty about them is that they give the impression that Berkeley is defending doctrines he is on the point of disowning. Berkeley is not defending them, but is at pains to show that they are not so absurd as they seem, and that they have been in fact held by thinkers of various schools. It is as if he said, If I were to hold and teach intermittency and the companion doctrines, which you call absurd, I should be in good company ; for they are freely taught in both the old philosophy and the new. These are not absurd doctrines, though I do not say they are mine. Locke and Descartes teach that light and colours " are meer sensations that exist no longer than they are perceived " ; the Schoolmen explain the divine conservation as a continual creation ; and even if we grant the existence of matter, we do not escape intermittency ; for the supposed matter has to be infinitely divisible, void of figure and size. What then of the particular bodies we see and touch, with their shapes and sizes ? Where do they stand ? The matterist has to admit that on his own theory they arise with perception, vary with it, and cease when it ceases.[1]

In section 48 Berkeley bids us take a bird's-eye view of the perceptual situation as a whole. As long as we take partial views, and confine our attention to individual seeing and touching, a case for intermittency can be made

---

[1] Berkeley was a keen tactician, and he may have hoped that his restraint would conciliate a body of neutral opinion (see *PC* 406), the Cambridge Platonists, followers of Malebranche and Norris, men who did not deny matter nor affirm it strongly. Thinkers who distrusted the senses and sought truth in the supersensible sphere alone would be attracted rather than otherwise by the " pretended absurdities " of intermittency, etc.

out. If my perception of this red colour be taken as a complete self-contained space-time event (which it is *not*), then, in a sense, the colour I see may be said to cease when I cease to see it, and to be re-created, or otherwise resuscitated, when I see it again. But why take it so ? Why should the philosopher take the part for the whole ? Reintegrate the part in its space-time context. Leave the lower levels of psychology and the merely subjective processes of perception. Climb with Berkeley here to the heights. Thence see my perception as a real but tiny part of a cosmic scheme. Objects which from below are " my ideas," from a height are " our ideas," and from the highest height are God's ideas. We do not make them ; we receive them. God gives them, or offers them. From the lofty standpoint the case for intermittency, real objective intermittency, collapses like a house of cards. If there be a spiritual Substance of the universe, with power matching knowledge, if there be a spiritual bond between finite spirits, as clearly there is, then the object of sense can be handed on from man to man, like the torch in the torch-race. You can perceive my ideas of sense, and I yours ; for neither of us makes what we both see. And when neither you, nor I, nor any other created spirit, perceives the object, it is still there, still luminous, still significant, still perceived, still in the mind of God. That is a free rendering of Berkeley's final answer to this objection ; there you have his full account of the perceivable. " For thô we hold indeed the objects of sense to be nothing else but ideas which cannot exist unperceived ; yet we may not hence conclude they have no existence except only while they are perceived by us, since there may be some other spirit that perceives them thô we do not. Wherever bodies are said to have no existence without the mind, I would not be understood to mean this or that particular mind, but all minds whatsoever."

That clear statement disposes of the fourth objection, and, incidentally, of solipsist and subjectivist interpretations of the *esse est percipi*. It duly *places* the perceivable in the Berkeleian metaphysic ; for what I perceive is, thus, perceivable by you, and what is perceivable by you and me is perceived by God.

Objection V (§ 49)

" If extension and figure exist only in the mind, it follows that the mind is extended and figured."

Berkeley deals with the objection summarily, but he had considered it carefully,[1] and it elicits an important statement on the nature of existence in the mind.

Space does not " infect " the mind. The mind does not become spatial by thinking of space ; spatial objects are in the mind as objects of mind, not as mental objects. Spatial qualities, says Berkeley, " are in the mind only as they are perceived by it, that is, not by way of mode or attribute, but only by way of *idea*." I can think of round or square or large or small, and my mind does not become round or square or large or small. I can see red, white, and blue without developing a coloured mind. Those objects are " in the mind " only " by way of idea," *i.e.* as objects minded, as objects which do not qualify the subject.

Interpretations of Berkeley's key doctrine are true or false, according as they conform, or otherwise, to this pronouncement. The *esse est percipi* does not cut across

[1] See *PC* 878 and my note there.

the subject-object relation. Berkeley is loyal to that relation through thick and thin. In perception subject remains subject, and object remains object, and there is no mixing or confounding of natures. The mind remains the mind, and does not become what is in the mind ; nor does what is in the mind partake in the qualities of the mind. The active and passive do not share. Idealist interpretations of Berkeley's philosophy place his sensible world in the mind " by way of mode or attribute," *i.e.* as Spinoza's space is in Spinoza's god ; and that is just the view of things which Berkeley here disclaims and refutes.

Objections VI and X (§§ 50, 58–59)

" Whatever advances have been made, either by ancient or modern philosophers, in the study of nature do all proceed on the supposition, that corporeal substance or matter doth really exist."

" The notions we advance are inconsistent with several sound truths in philosophy and mathematics."

Berkeley replies that matter does not really enter into scientific explanations ; for there is nothing nominally explained by matter which could not equally well be explained without it. To explain phenomena is to show how we are affected by ideas. Matter cannot produce ideas in a spirit, and therefore matter can explain nothing.

The other objection seems to have been added to enable Berkeley to deal *ad hoc* with the motion of the earth—an outstanding instance of " unperceived motion." The gist of Berkeley's reply is that unperceived motion is not motion out of mind, but motion perceivable. Thus

when we say that the earth moves, though we do not
see it move, we simply mean that if we were placed in
such or such a position we should see the earth move
" among the choir of the planets."

Objection VII (§§ 51–53)

> " We must no longer say upon these principles
> that fire heats or water cools, but that a spirit
> heats, &c. Would not a man be deservedly
> laughed at who should talk after this
> manner ? "

Yes, says Berkeley ; he would. Do not talk so, but
think so. " In such things we ought to think with the
learned, and speak with the vulgar." Language is based
on practice, and inaccurate modes of speech are in
practice necessary. Copernicans, for instance, have to
speak of the sun rising and setting.

The question of fact depends, of course, on the truth,
or otherwise, of Berkeley's doctrine of cause.[1] What he
teaches has much in common with common sense and with
the teaching of the " regularity " school. Many types of
so-called causes are obviously no more than regular
sequences of signs, quite devoid of agency ; and when
in ordinary life we speak of the fire heating the pot, or
the water cooling the horse-shoe, we are not really ascribing operation to inanimate things. We are indeed recognizing the presence of activity and change ; but we
are not saying anything about the activity, and our
meaning is simply that changes are occurring in accordance with the universal laws of nature, changes which

---

[1] See Chapter IX.

will enable me in a few minutes to make the tea or fit the shoe ; but we do not say (and I, for one, certainly do not mean) that those bickering tongues of flame or those quiet drops of water are agents which make the changes begin to be.

When one considers the heating and the cooling as part of a world-wide scheme and process, it becomes impossible for the thinker to regard those changes as the work of little, local agents ; the agency must be viewed, as Berkeley claims, on a cosmic scale as the settled law of operation of the one great moving Spirit.

Berkeley notes that some of the Schoolmen and some " moderns," *i.e.* Malebranche and the occasionalists, have taught that there are no corporeal causes ; but, he complains, they have not gone the whole way with reason ; they have halted at an untenable position (like many theists to-day). Accepting the passivity of all objects of sense, they go on to argue for the existence of passive, material archetypes, which do nothing and serve no purpose in the divine economy—" a very unaccountable and extravagant supposition."

Objections VIII and IX   (§§ 54–57)

" Must we suppose the whole world to be mistaken, and if so, what cause can be assigned of so wide-spread and predominant an error ? "

Berkeley denies that matter is backed by universal consent. He says that, strictly speaking, men cannot *believe* in what involves a contradiction (*e.g.* insensible sense data) or is meaningless (*e.g.* material substance). It is true that men act as if the immediate cause of their sensations " were some senseless unthinking being," but they do not know what they mean by those words, and have no " settled speculative opinion " corresponding to them.

Again, suppose that universal consent were conceded in this case, for the sake of discussion ; that is a poor argument for its truth. Few outside the ranks of learning believe in the antipodes or the motion of the earth.

The prevalence of matterism can be explained as a joint-product of ignorance and sophistication. The vulgar realize that they themselves are not the authors of their ideas of sense, and they attribute to those ideas " an existence independent of and without the mind." Philosophers go part of the way with the vulgar ; for they know that they are not the cause of their own sensations ; further, they correct the mistake of the vulgar to the extent of admitting that the objects we immediately perceive are in the mind ; but instead of stopping there they proceed to manufacture the impossible theory of dual existence, and invent objects outside the mind, supposed to resemble those within the mind, and supposed to cause them.

Objection XI (§§ 60–66)

" To what purpose serves that curious organisation of plants and the admirable mechanism in the parts of animals."

Berkeley accepts mechanisms and organizations ; his system does not require or indeed permit us to hold that things exist in surface only ; he accepts and justifies the hidden parts of things and nature's secrets. The question, for him, is not whether the apparatus exists, but what purpose it serves. If nature's actions are God's actions, why does not the divine Artist produce His results directly, without the aid of apparatus ?

He begins by pointing out that to the matterist who believes in God this difficulty is insuperable. The matterist must regard the apparatus in question as outside the mind ; man never sees or touches it or gets any good of it. He has therefore to suppose that God has made all this infinity of things, called material, *idly* ; they do nothing and serve no purpose for God or man. Material mechanisms are inexplicable. Sensible mechanisms, on the other hand, can be readily explained by the immaterialist ; for they, unlike the supposed material mechanisms, lie well within the range of mind ; the inner parts and structure of plants and animals are visible and tangible ; the biologist understands them ; they do nothing actively, but they serve the turn of expert and inexpert ; they teach us what to do ; they teach us the ways of God's working ; they furnish the elements of human knowledge, and being the expressions of divine law and order, they have their place in the scheme of things. They are not " absolutely necessary," but they are " necessary to the producing of things in a constant, regular way, according to the laws of nature." Knowledge and action depend on the uniformity of nature and conformity to law. God could produce the motions on the dial of a watch without the action of the " works " or the help of the watchmaker. But were He to do so, the art of watchmaking would not exist, and the watchmaker would not know how to make or mend a watch. The same applies to all the arts and sciences. The rules and principles governing man's action and his science depend on his use of the sensible apparatus and the mechanisms given by God.

On these principles Berkeley gives a rational explanation of miracle. God can overrule His own rules. All natural events are works of God ; miracles are His exceptional works, actions done out of the ordinary course, done for good reasons, above law, but not against it.

Objection XII (§§ 67–81)

" There may, perhaps, be some inert, unperceiving substance, or substratum of some other qualities, as incomprehensible to us as colours are to a man born blind, because we have not a sense adapted to them."

In this long section Berkeley deals with the agnostic or semi-agnostic defences of matter set up in his day. Most of them depend on the notion of the " occasion," which is no longer a living issue ; but the argument from the " sixth sense " is still influential.

Berkeley gives, first, a smart answer, and then a solid answer. If we do not know what matter is, if it is only an unknown support of unknown qualities, clearly " it's no matter whether there is such a thing or no." This little jest, almost certainly conscious, is an interesting anticipation of Byron's *mot* to the effect that if Berkeley said there is no matter, it is no matter what Berkeley said.

Coming to grips with the objection, Berkeley urges that if we had a new sense, " it could only furnish us with new ideas or sensations," and to them his previous arguments would apply ; if the data of the five senses can exist only in the mind, the same would hold of the data of the " sixth sense." A new sense could yield new objects for the mind, but could not possibly yield objects outside the range of mind.

Objection XIII (§§ 82–84)

" The Holy Scriptures are so clear in the point, as will sufficiently convince every good Christian, that bodies do really exist, and are something more than meer ideas."

This is obviously a special case of the first objection. It rests on the common confusion between matter and sensible body, and assumes that Berkeley is using the term *idea* in the colloquial or representationist way.

Berkeley asserts, as before, the real existence of sensible bodies, and justly claims that his doctrine could not conflict with writings, sacred or profane, which do likewise. He is willing to accept " even corporeal substances, when taken in the vulgar sense " ; but, he adds truly enough, neither matter nor the existence of objects without the mind are anywhere mentioned in Scripture.

CHAPTER XII

THE CONSEQUENCES AND THE KNOWING
OF KNOWING

(*Principles*, §§ 85 to the end)[1]

In the second half of the *Principles* Berkeley considers his
" tenets in their consequences," showing that his denial
of matter is no mere negation, but leads to a positive
philosophy of sense and spirit. I can attempt to cover
half the book in one chapter only because my main
business is with Berkeley's immaterialism ; where his
immaterialism makes good, its consequences will take
care of themselves. The *Principles* as a denial of matter
is a complete work, and a work of art ; as an exposition
of the consequences of immaterialism it is a torso. All
we have is Part I ; a considerable portion of Part II
was written and lost ; Part III was planned only.[2] His
other works, notably his *Essay on Vision*, have been very
influential, but his permanent contribution to the main
stream of philosophical thought is his denial of matter
with the closely connected doctrines contained in the
first thirty-three sections of the *Principles*.

I have added " THE KNOWING OF KNOWING " to
the chapter title because in these seventy-two sections
Berkeley redeems to some extent the promise of his
title, and shows how immaterialism affects human

[1] A draft of the greater part is contained in the notebook, now in the
British Museum, classed as Add. MS. 39304, pp. 35–105 ; the variants
between this draft and the text of the first edition are given in Jessop's
edition of the *Principles*.
[2] See *PC* 508, 676, with my notes.

knowledge in the spheres of theology, psychology, and the sciences.

Berkeley's objects of knowledge fall into four classes or two. The four-fold classing yields the analysis :

§§ 85–134   Knowledge of ideas
§§ 135–144   Knowledge of the self
§ 145   Knowledge of other minds
§§ 146–end   Knowledge of God

If we follow the classing suggested by Berkeley (§ 86), the analysis is twofold, *viz.*

§§ 85–134   Knowledge of ideas
§§ 135–end   Knowledge of spirits

Under knowledge of ideas Berkeley treats of scepticism, of the general features of sensible things, *viz.* time, space, and number, and of the sciences thereon founded, arithmetic and geometry. He has criticisms of the Newtonian physics and of infinitesimals.

As regards the self, his aim is to establish the reality of self-knowledge, while distinguishing it sharply from our knowledge of sensible things. On our knowledge of other minds he has only one section, which looks hurried and incomplete. It is concerned with a technicality which has a bearing on our knowledge of God.

The sections on our knowledge of God form a masterly exposition of reasoned belief in Deity. It is the crown and completion of the philosophy. I will sketch Berkeley's treatment of these topics, following his order.

ASSURANCE OR SCEPTICISM (§§ 85–96)

Berkeley mentions three problems of his day which automatically disappear with the disappearance of matter.

These are : the possibility of matter's thinking (*Locke*, IV iii 6), the infinite divisibility of matter, and the action of matter upon spirit. The first of these appears to-day in discussions as to whether mind could evolve out of matter ; the other two, though not *live* issues, are still uncriticized assumptions of much contemporary thought. The disappearance of these problems simplifies the task of philosophy, and helps to substitute assurance for intellectual " dither and wobble."

He then powerfully argues that matter is " the very root of scepticism." Matterism postulates " a twofold existence of the objects of sense, the one *intelligible*, or in the mind, the other *real* and without the mind." This duplication of the world and of every single thing in it puts a palsy in the thinker's mind. He tries and tries again to consider sensible and material as existing side by side, like Humpty and Dumpty ; he tries and tries again to consider the material as real and the sensible as unreal ; both notions are too ridiculous for words. Matter can never be brought into comparison, and therefore can never serve as a criterion of real knowledge ; if it exists, the agreement between it and our " ideas " can never be ascertained ; and we must fold our hands, and " sit down in a forelorn scepticism." (Introd. § 1)

Berkeley's assurance springs from his New Principle. Since *esse* is *percipi*, " colour, figure, motion, extension, and the like, considered only as so many sensations in the mind, are perfectly known, there being nothing in them which is not perceived." These striking words apply to any and every case of sense perception. Berkeley is claiming direct awareness and full awareness. This pink patch, that sweet smell, this circle, that square, and the swift sparkle of yonder meteor can be taken at their face value ; they are what they seem ; they are " perfectly

known " ; for they are here before me in my mind, and
all in.   Sense your sensations, says Berkeley ;   perceive
your perceptions.   He knows that the functioning of one
sense is " complicated " with that of another, that memory
and anticipation qualify our sensings and that possible
sensations fringe the actual.   He knows all that, and finds
a place for it in his philosophy ; but he insists that what
is in my mind is in my mind, and I cannot be mistaken
about it.   There is always more to learn in subsequent
sensings ; but the beginning of wisdom about an actual
sensation is the principle that what I see and touch I
see and touch ; it is, *pro tanto*, all that is there to see and
touch ; the bogey of matter is laid ; material archetypes
have melted like a morning mist ; the object of sense
is " perfectly known."

As against scepticism Berkeley erects " a firm system
of sound and real knowledge."   He gives a summary of his
tenets in sections 89–91, and in it should be noted the
sharp contrast he draws between spirits and ideas, and
his firm belief in both.   His ensuing statement on externality is also important.   He still rejects, of course, external
things interpreted to mean material things, things in the
outer darkness of an incomprehensible somewhat ;   but
he affirms external things in the ordinary sense of the
term ; he affirms things other than ourselves, things of
external origin, and he rejects in terms the view that
the things perceived by sense are " generated from within,
by the mind itself."   An external world, so composed, is
a public world, a world in which we all may share, and
not private and personal to the individual ; and Berkeley
draws attention to this fact in his words here, " Thus
when I shut my eyes, the things I saw may still exist,
but it must be in another mind."

TIME (§§ 97, 98)

Time [1] is introduced here as one of the subjects touched by the dead hand of abstraction. Far from wishing to idealize time, Berkeley wishes us to take it in the concrete, as the series of experienced events. St. Augustine was asked what time was, and he said he knew till he was asked. He meant that concrete time is familiar to all of us, but that time in the abstract is an insoluble mystery. That is the gist of Berkeley's contention here. Let us develop his illustration.

Bid your servant to meet you at two o'clock at Nelson's Pillar or the Marble Arch. There is no difficulty about it ; both co-ordinates are real and known. " Two o'clock " is just as real and objective as the pillar or the arch. Time is a character or quality of the succession of ideas in our minds, and " two o'clock " is a measure of time indicating the occurrence of such and such an idea or conjunction of ideas. The " succession of ideas in our minds " does not mean a succession of mental events, but a succession of events thought, willed, and felt. Time is that concrete flow which we feel in our bones and watch in events. We call it transience. Berkeleian time is your day and my day, this year, next year ; it is the passing of sights and sounds, the blast of the wind, the flow of the stream, the ticking of the clock ; it is the pulse and the heart-beat, the sigh and the song, the before, between, and after of concrete experience. It is in " all those particular actions and ideas that diversifie

---

[1] Berkeley's thoughts on time were intimately connected with the beginnings of his immaterialism. " One of my earliest inquiries was about time," he wrote to his American friend, Johnson. This early study is reflected in the opening pages of his *Commentaries*, where time is one of the indexed subjects. See Nos. 4 and 9 with my notes there, and Fraser, *Works* (1901), vol. ii, pp. 19–20.

the day." It is the time that we live, the homely *now* and *then* of the " passing show." We might call it Bergson's " *durée* " without those semi-mystical qualities he reads into it.

If we want a different sort of time, some majestic framework of cosmic history, a time that is other than its contents, if we want a time we impose but do not find, a time we conceive or imagine but do not live, then, Berkeley holds, we are passing from concrete thinking to abstract thinking. If we define time as " the continuation of existence, or duration in abstract," we make it incomprehensible, and the source of absurdities.

The infinite divisibility of time is one such absurdity, Berkeley holds ; for when applied to personal existence it leads to absurd consequences. If the time I live be infinitely divisible, then I must pass innumerable ages without a thought, or I must be annihilated every moment of my life. I am waiting for my servant at the rendezvous and I hear the clock strike two. Between these two strokes an infinity of moments must elapse, if time be infinitely divisible. What then am I during that interval which seems so short and, on this theory, is so long ? Am I in a trance, animation and all my activities being suspended ? Am I nothing at all, annihilated when the first stroke dies away and returning to consciousness when the second stroke begins ? It is an absurd dilemma, and the theory which involves those alternatives stands condemned. Berkeley takes the point as proved, and proceeds to draw the inferences that (1) Time is nothing apart from the succession of ideas in our minds.[1] (2) Our duration is long or short, as our ideas or actions are many or few. (3) The soul always thinks.[2]

---

[1] In the *Commentaries* (4) he says that time is the succession ; he puts it more guardedly here.   [2] *Ct. Locke*, II i 10.

The question has been raised as to whether Berkeley can admit a public or common time. The answer is, I think, that he not only can but does admit it.[1] He does not deal with the question *ad hoc*; it was no question to him; it is a question forced on him by false, solipsist interpretations of his general outlook and teaching. His first interest, naturally, is the time of his own inner consciousness; but he was no solipsist about successive ideas, any more than he was about co-existing ideas; neither space nor time shuts him up in a narrow personal circle. In this very passage he speaks indifferently of the succession in *my mind* and in *our minds*. And of course no solipsist would choose the illustration he chooses. To bid your servant meet you at such a time is to assume the existence of a time common to two minds, and if to two minds, why not to all? Berkeley, good empiricist that he is, appeals constantly to his reader's personal experience, and naturally he stresses at times the private aspects of personal experience; but that stress is quite consistent with belief in a public space-time continuum perceived. There are many currents of consciousness, many eddies of events, many streams of experience in the one river of public time.

NEWTONIAN PHYSICS (§§ 101–117)

Berkeley charges the physicists of his day with adopting the principles of scepticism. He takes exception to

---

[1] The words here " which . . . is participated by all beings " are indecisive; grammatically, they may refer either to the simple idea of time which he rejects, or to the succession of ideas which he affirms. The latter is the more natural way of reading the passage. Even if it refers to the Newtonian absolute time, which Berkeley rejects, it by no means follows that he rejected that particular aspect of it. Newton has somewhere a phrase like " which flows uniformly ", used of time, but I cannot find the quotation now.

the mistrust of the senses shown in their assertion, " something there is, in every drop of water, every grain of sand, which it is beyond the power of human understanding, to fathom or comprehend." [1] He then makes a frontal attack on Newton's doctrines of attraction, and of space, time, and motion.

Newton's law of gravitation assumes the existence of matter, and in so far as it does so, it is, Berkeley teaches, " a vain circle, concluding in truth no more than this —that gravity is proportionable to weight, that is, to itself." [2] The term *attraction* describes the phenomena, the fall of the stone, the flow of the tide, the cohesion of bodies, etc., but does not indicate *how* each is done, nor explain it, nor name the cause. There is no efficient cause other than mind or spirit. Physicists do not know the causes of phenomena better than other folk, but having a larger compass of mind, they are able to reduce to rule a larger number of phenomena, and thus they are in a better position to explain the past and predict the future. But these powers must be used with caution ; the laws of nature are neither necessary nor universal ; there are exceptions, for instance, to the law of gravitation, such as the rise of sap and the elasticity of the air. The laws of nature are descriptions of the ways in which bodies behave, and their behaviour depends entirely on the will of God.

Newton's doctrine of space, time, and motion exemplifies, for Berkeley, the disastrous effects of abstract

[1] Those who resolve appearances into mechanical causes are the followers of Locke and Boyle. Those who account for them by " occult qualities " are probably Plato, Aristotle, Hippocrates, Scaliger, and Henry More, whose principles are listed in *PC* 617, " anima mundi, substantial forms, omniscient radical heat, plastic vertue, hylarchic principle." This list occurs again in the third of the *Three Dialogues, ad fin* ; it was probably taken over from Cheyne, *Philos. Princ. Natural Religion*, p. 3.

[2] *Siris* 319 ; *cf. PC* 361 and my note *ib.*

thinking. Concrete space and motion we all know, just as we know concrete time ; they are relative quanta, characters of sense data, *e.g.* the spread of colour or the flash of a shooting star. No one ever doubts space or motion, so conceived. Space is the togetherness or co-existence of ideas, and motion is their perceived movement. But when the faculty of abstraction has done its work, and has first abstracted, *e.g.* space from colour, and then the *existence* of space from perceived space, this " twofold abstraction " (§ 99) makes us lose sight of real space and motion, and " run into great extravagancies." Thus the habit of abstraction has made Newton duplicate all three quanta ; he postulates absolute space, absolute time, and absolute motion, side by side with relative space, relative time, and relative motion. Here, objects Berkeley, are represented to my mind, pairs of entities, each pair under one name, space, time, and motion ; yet there are, we are told, two types of space, two types of time, and two types of motion. I can conceive no relation whatsoever between the two entities which bear the one name. These supposed absolutes " are ordinarily conceived with relation to sensible things, to which, nevertheless, in their own nature, they bear no relation at all."

Turning to detailed criticism, Berkeley concentrates on motion. Absolute motion, according to Newton, is the translation of a body from absolute place to absolute place—place being that part of space which is occupied by any body—and five distinctions between absolute motion and relative are laid down. In reply Berkeley urges that the only conceivable motion is relative ; it takes two bodies to make a motion, though it is not necessary that both should be moved ; if there were but one body in existence, it could not be moved ; for there would be no body from which it could vary its distance. Thus, for Berkeley, the essence of motion is variation of perceived distance, while, for Newton, it is translation in unperceived space. The latter doctrine is diametrically opposed to the *esse est percipi*. Berkeley takes pains to prove that relative motion is not necessarily unreal. When I walk over stones, for instance, I move, but the stones only seem to move. The distinguishing mark between real relative motion and apparent is the application of force to the body moved.

Berkeley explains the supposed demand for absolute motion as a demand for a standard of relative motion, *i.e.* a fixed criterion of rest and motion. A man on ship may be both at rest and in motion, at rest with regard to the ship, but moving with regard to the land. In the ordinary affairs of life we take the earth to be at rest, and judge motion with respect to it ; but philosophers know that the earth is moved, and they must seek a more remote standard ; accordingly they let their thoughts away to " the utmost, unmoved walls," which they take to be the measure of true motion. Carry the quest a stage further, and you reach the concept of absolute motion ; but absolute motion in the strict sense is inconceivable ; there is no such thing ; and the experiment of the water in the rotating vessel, supposed to prove it, is vitiated by a mistaken reading of the facts.

Berkeley claims to have already refuted absolute time (§§ 97–98), and of course both it and absolute space disappear if absolute motion goes. " Pure space " [1] is only another name for absolute space.

---

[1] On pure space see *PC* 135, 298, and my notes there ; also Berkeley's letter to Johnson of 24th March 1730, Fraser, *Works* (1901), vol. ii, p. 19.

MATHEMATICS (§§ 118–134)

With regard to arithmetic, Berkeley's aim is to show that the science does not rest on abstract ideas [1] of unity or of numbers, and that the mysterious properties assigned to those abstractions has set an artificial value upon trifling speculations. Arithmetic originated in the practical need for counting. At first men used strokes or points ; then on the analogy of letters figures were invented. Numbers, like letters, are signs, and we can sum, divide, and proportion the things signified because of the established connections between them and the signs. The signs have no intrinsic value ; they do not represent abstract numbers ; their simple purpose is to guide our actions in practical affairs ; they do not lead to speculative truth.

On geometry [2] Berkeley has two things to say ; first, that its subject-matter is neither absolute space, nor pure space, nor the abstract idea of space, and therefore must be the concrete space of experience, the visible and tangible line or surface ; and, secondly, that the space of geometry is not infinitely divisible.[3] The second point follows from the first.

The wording of Berkeley's thesis should be noted ; he undertakes to prove that " no finite extension contains innumerable parts or is infinitely divisible " (§ 123). He uses three lines of proof and mentions a fourth. Infinite

[1] See *PC* 762, 766, 803, and *Locke*, II vii 7 and IV vi.
[2] *Cf. PC* 101 and my note there, and *TV* 150ff.
[3] The infinite divisibility of space was assumed in the works of almost all the leading mathematicians of the period—Barrow, Keil, Cheyne, etc. Great speculative importance was attached to it, and arguments were founded upon it. Pierre Bayle was a notable exception, and I think that some of the articles in his dictionary (especially *Pyrrho* and *Zeno*) had considerable influence upon Berkeley. A great deal of attention is devoted to infinite divisibility in the *Commentaries*, see my note on No. 11.

divisibility (1) conflicts with the New Principle (§ 124), (2) is based on the doctrine of abstract ideas (§§ 125–26), (3) is a case of false substitution (§§ 126–28), and (4) leads to absurd consequences (§ 129).

The argument from the New Principle is as follows : a finite extension is an extension seen or touched ; it is an idea ; I perceive it ; it is here before me in my mind ; therefore I know it perfectly ; it is an object of sense, and there is nothing in it which cannot be sensed. The finite line or surface, seen or touched, cannot contain innumerable parts which *ex hypothesi* cannot be seen or touched. The same holds of imagined extension. I can imagine an *infinite* line infinitely divisible or containing infinite parts. I cannot imagine a *finite* line infinitely divisible or containing infinite parts. Since then I cannot see, touch, or imagine infinite parts in a finite line, I conclude they are not there.

The arguments from abstraction and substitution work in together and form a psychological explanation of the false reasoning which misleads the geometrician. The finite line which you imagine to be infinitely divisible is not real extension, but an abstract idea. The geometrician when he is demonstrating about universals (Introduction, § xv) is in fact dealing with the particular lines, figures, etc., in the diagram which he has before his eyes or his mind's eye ; but he treats them as universals by neglecting their particularities, such as size. He does not form an abstract idea of them, as Locke thinks, but takes each line or figure in its representative aspect, supposing it to stand for innumerable other lines or figures. So far, so good ; but this legitimate representation readily passes into illegitimate substitution. The geometrician takes a short line AB, an inch long, and makes it stand for a long line XY, a mile long. AB can represent XY, but when the geometrician goes further, and mentally substitutes the one for the other, and supposes them to correspond in detail, the door is open for infinite divisibility. AB, an inch long, does not contain 10,000 parts ; XY, a mile long, does contain 10,000 parts ; but when AB is substituted for XY, the properties of the long line, including that of possessing 10,000 parts, are mentally transferred to the short line ; thus the visible line on paper before you becomes credited with possessing invisible parts ; if you imagine it to possess 10,000 parts, you may as well go further and imagine it to possess an infinite number of parts.

Finally, Berkeley glances at " the several absurdities and contradictions which flowed from this false principle." [1]

Infinitesimals [2] are next considered (§§ 130–134). Some held that finite lines can be divided into infinitesimal parts, and stopped there ; others went further and held that each infinitesimal in its turn can be divided into infinitesimals of the second order, and so on *ad infinitum*. Berkeley argues that both parties are wrong ; for there is no such thing as a part infinitely small, nor can there be an infinite number of parts in any finite quantity. Lines and figures can be measured and their properties ascertained without the supposition of infinitesimals. Minute and almost insensible quantities may be named infinitesimals, but at bottom they are

[1] See *PC* 322, 364, 877.
[2] Preparatory studies by Wallis (*PC* 482, 837) had been brought to fruition by Newton and Leibniz. Berkeley's earliest extant philosophical work, the tract *Of Infinites*, deals with the subject, and so do several entries in the *Commentaries*, *e.g.* No. 308. He originally planned a fuller treatment, but here he is content to give those " hints to the public " of which he speaks twenty-five years later in the *Analyst* (§ 50), and which he developed there and in his *Defence of Free-thinking* and *Reasons for Not Replying*.

finite ; for there cannot be quantities smaller than the *minimum sensibile*.[1]

SELF-KNOWLEDGE (§§ 135-144)

The attempt to prove the existence of mind or spirit [2] is apt to defeat itself, and Berkeley wisely does not make the attempt. He assumes that we know our own minds as we know our own bodies. He takes his stand on the two given realities, mind and body, and does not argue with those who deny either. His immaterialism greatly simplifies the problem of self-knowledge. If there is no matter, there is no problem of mind and matter. Mind being active and body passive, there is no attempt to derive the one from the other ; there is no interaction, for body cannot act ; there is no parallelism, for no parallel can be drawn between that which acts and the passive. Mind and body do not merge or blend, but there is no necessary antagonism between them. They are meant to harmonize and agree. They are adapted to each other, since creative Mind gives both.

In his earlier section (27) Berkeley was concerned with the spirit as active cause ; in these sections he is stressing the reality of self-knowledge and its distinctness

---

[1] Berkeley's conception of the *minimum sensibile*, perhaps tracing to Cavalieri's " indivisibles " (*PC* 346), receives a great deal of attention in the *Commentaries* (see my note on No. 59), and is several times referred to in the *Essay on Vision* (54, 79ff). This is the only mention of it in the *Principles*. The *minimum sensibile* (*visibile, tangibile*) is Berkeley's answer to the mathematical point, supposed infinitely divisible. There are difficulties in the conception, of which Berkeley was conscious, and he may have thought it more prudent to refrain from detailed exposition. He has said enough to show that he believed in an objective, external world, composed of sensible *minima*, and the heart of his contention about them is that the senses ought to be trusted about things sensible.

[2] The two terms are used indifferently in Berkeley's works, but on the whole *spirit* is the more characteristic as more expressive of activity.

from other types of knowledge. Some in his day had formed an ideal of self-knowledge which in clarity and richness would approximate to geometrical knowledge, and failing to realize this ideal had become sceptics about the soul. Berkeley traced this scepticism to the Lockian doctrine of the idea of the soul, and proceeds to give his reasons for denying that we have any idea of soul or spirit in the strict use of the term *idea*. I need not repeat what was said above (pp. 97–99) on this important denial, the delicate situation it creates, and the steps which Berkeley took in both editions to obviate misunderstanding. But a new point is raised in section 140 [1] on which something must be said.

There are two senses, says Berkeley, in which we may legitimately speak of an idea of the soul. First, there is the " large " or colloquial sense, in which " I have an idea of" is simply a long-winded way of saying "I know." But in another sense also (not a very natural sense) the phrase may be justified. My spirit is like your spirit, and to that extent may be called an idea or image of it —not that pictures of spirits can be formed, but that analogical reasoning holds from the one to the other. Your spirit bears the same relation to my spirit as the blue you see bears to the blue I see. The point is not of much intrinsic importance ; but this likeness between spirits enters into Berkeley's epistemology as being the basis of the analogical reasoning by which we pass from self-knowledge to knowledge of other minds or spirits, and thence to the knowledge of God.

Self-knowledge, for Berkeley, is real knowledge, but it differs in kind from knowledge of ideas. *How*, then, do

[1] The section is clumsily constructed and badly punctuated, and has the appearance of an afterthought. Jessop points out in his note *ad loc.* that in the MS. it is on the left-hand facing page, reserved for additions and corrections.

we know the self? What is the manner, the peculiarity, of self-knowledge? Berkeley does not characterize it positively in the first edition, but he repairs this omission subsequently. In the third of the *Three Dialogues* (*ad init.*) he contrasts it with other types of knowledge, calling it *immediate, intuitive,* and by *reflex act.*[1] In the *De Motu* (§21) we find the interesting term for it, *conscientia quadam interna.*[2] In the second edition of the *Principles* (§ 88) is added, " We comprehend our own existence by inward feeling [3] or reflexion, and that of other spirits by reason." Thus self-knowledge is distinguished not only from knowledge of ideas, but from knowledge of other minds, and Berkeley virtually accepts Malebranche's contention that it is non-ideational, and uses the equivalent of Malebranche's term for it, *conscience.*[4] He holds that we are not, *in full,* objects to ourselves. We cannot place the total self, as it were, under the microscope of introspection, and exclude all else. We know ourselves ; we know ourselves immediately, but partially, dimly perhaps, and along with other objects.

Berkeley says that " the natural immortality of the soul " is a consequence of his doctrine, not in the sense that the soul is absolutely indestructible, but that the ordinary processes of change and decay do not affect it. He means that God could withdraw the living life He gave if the soul ceased to want to exist, or ceased to deserve to exist, but that sickness, dissolution, and death, being changes in passive things, cannot touch the active core of being.

[1] " by reflexion," 3rd ed. addition to this passage.
[2] *Cf. Alc.* vii 5.
[3] See my note on *PC* 888.
[4] *Cf.* " introversion," *PC* 539, the seventeenth-century equivalent of introspection, and " I have some knowledge or notion of my mind." *Princ.* 142, 2nd ed.

KNOWLEDGE OF OTHER MINDS (§ 145)

Locke has a few remarks about it (IV iii 17, xi 9-12), and Malebranche (III ii 7) treats it as a specific type of knowledge ; but Berkeley found little to help him about it in these authorities, and he seems to have been more or less feeling his way. There is one reference to it in the *Commentaries* (No. 752), and in the *Principles*, besides this section, we have a few scattered remarks in sections 140, 147, and 148.[1] Perhaps Berkeley decided to give here just the bare bones of his theory, and to leave fuller discussion over for his Part II. Whatever the reason, his treatment is summary and sketchy ; he does not take the issue squarely on its merits, and he seems concerned with it chiefly as an element in his account of man's knowledge of God. What he says here is put more technically in the third of the *Three Dialogues* (*ad init.*), where he cleverly connects it with knowledge of ideas, of the self, and of God.[2]

Berkeley argues that this type of knowledge is mediate and inferential. It involves self-reference and sense perception, and is virtually an argument from analogy. We might put it this way : I hear your laugh ; it is like the noise I make when I am amused, and therefore it can serve as the basis of an inference from my mind to your mind. As my laugh is to my mind, so is my hearing of your laugh to my perception of your mind.

Someone has said that we do not want " inferred friends " ; our wants and wishes do not decide these things, of course ; but certainly the inferential theory by itself does seem artificial. Our knowledge of other minds

---

[1] The MS. breaks off abruptly in the middle of § 145 ; if that is anything to go by, we might infer that a change of mind or of plan occurred.

[2] See also *Alc.* iv 5, where Euphranor analyses his awareness of Alciphron.

is too quick for a laboured process of deduction, too warm and intimate for a cold-blooded inference. In actual life there is an almost immediate recognition of kind, an instinctive, semi-physiological recognition of the other self as the brother self. And I think Berkeley virtually admits that there is this other side to the question when he comes to integrate this type of knowledge with a higher type. He denies (§ 145) that our knowledge of other minds is " immediate, as is the knowledge of my ideas," and yet he says (§ 147) that " God is known as certainly and immediately as any other mind or spirit whatsoever distinct from ourselves." The two statements are not in flat contradiction, for both are qualified ; but in admitting degrees of immediacy, Berkeley does seem to be recognizing, consciously or unconsciously, the difficulty attending the inferential theory when it is applied in actual life.

KNOWLEDGE OF GOD (§§ 146-156)

Berkeley's account here of our knowledge of God is much more than an argument for His existence. It is that, but it is also an explanation, along novel lines, of the very character of that knowledge. He begins from the causal argument, sketched in section 29, marshals the many lines of teleological thought which lead Godward —reason, regularity, order, greatness, the instinct of animals, adaptation, system, beauty, the laws of pleasure and pain, and the inner harmony of creation, and adds the *a priori* arguments from the rational attributes. Having thus assembled the causal, the teleological, and the *a priori* arguments in one conspect, he makes the reader not only see them, but feel them, by displaying our knowledge of God as a higher consciousness, of which those stock arguments are the halting expression. Many men carry that higher consciousness about with them for life, and Berkeley tells us, in effect, that there is nothing accidental about it ; this " God-consciousness," if we may so say, is no product of dream or myth, no result of religious education ; it is something in the main stream of life ; it is an extension of the vital, sentient, and rational processes which have yielded our knowledge of the *ego* and the *tu.*

We infer a human agent from the ideas or sensations they produce in us, and we go on to infer a divine agent from the " works of nature," for these are " the far greater part of the ideas or sensations perceived by us," and they are clearly " not produced by, or dependent on, the wills of men." As the works of nature are to the works of man, so is God to man, the infinite spirit to the finite. Technically this is inference, mediate knowledge ; for processes can be distinguished in it ; but the movement of thought is usually so quick and sure that Berkeley can call it " certain and immediate knowledge " ; it is like the passage from the written word to its meaning, practically instantaneous ; it is more like recognition than inference ; it dawns on the mind without twilight, like sunrise in eastern lands.

Warming to his theme, Berkeley asserts that " the existence of God is far more evidently perceived than the existence of men " ; for the works of nature are infinitely greater than the works of men. Indeed every mark or sign of a man is indirectly also a mark or sign of the divine operation. I can will to move my tongue to speak to you, or to put out my hand and touch you ; but that is all I can do. That these movements of mine should be to you significant signs, exciting ideas in your mind, is beyond my compass ; it depends wholly on the will of the Creator, who " maintains that intercourse between spirits, whereby they are able to perceive the existence of each other."

Here we have the authentic utterance of immaterialism; no matterist could conceive that eagle gaze. If God maintain that secret communion of minds which makes converse possible, then He is very close and our knowledge of Him is direct awareness, and inference to Him has become vision of Him. This is admitted by Berkeley, though cautiously. We may be said to *see* God, in a broad sense, because we divine His existence from what we see, as we divine the meaning of the printed page. We do not see Him " by a direct and immediate view." [1] We do not see representative ideas of corporeal things in the mind of God, as Malebranche taught; yet we *see* Him, as truly as we *see* a man. Berkeley is not making the invisible Spirit a visible God; he is seeing all things in God, and God in all things; for as we *see* the minds of our fellow men in the few small effects they have on us, so we *see* the Mind of nature in the works of nature. " Whithersoever we direct our view, we do at all times and in all places perceive manifest tokens of the Divinity." Thus the keystone of the great arch swings into place, and Berkeley's immaterialism is complete.

Berkeley's principles have their applications and uses on the lower levels of psychology and purely humanistic thought; but his immaterialism without God would be nonsense, and without a great God would be a weak and puny thing. Berkeley's denial of matter, when taken in its integrity, is an affirmation of a great God, and the Berkeleian philosophy attains its full strength and stature in the conception of a " spirit who is intimately present to our minds, producing in them all that variety of ideas

[1] *Cf.* " Jupiter est quodcunque vides."

or sensations, which continually affect us, on whom we have an absolute and intire dependence, in short, in whom we live and move and have our being." (§ 149.)

In the concluding sections (151-156) Berkeley glances at those difficulties, common to all forms of theism, which are eased, or appear to be eased, by the notion of nature as an active participant in events, and which appear to be heightened by the doctrine of the immediate presence and direct operation of God. Dysteleological events, roundabout methods of production, disorder, monsters, broken purposes, waste in nature, and the inherent miseries of human life—such things are hard to reconcile with the existence of a great and good God, and harder still to reconcile with His immediate operation. Volumes have been written on these problems, and of course Berkeley does not attempt an adequate treatment ; but in these pithy sections he has assembled the main principles of all theodicy, and has shown in outline how immaterialism can justify the ways of God to man.

We live our lives, he says in effect, within the framework of a system of rules, simple and general rules. The steady and consistent administration of those rules is proof of God's goodness and his wisdom. Government by general rules or laws is practically necessary, and is part of the education of the human faculties. " Particular inconveniences " must be interpreted in the light of the system. God's creation is a chequered pattern; it is light and shade, and the very defects and blemishes of which men complain serve to augment the beauty of the whole. Human conceptions of efficiency and thrift do not apply to the divine economy. What seems to us slowness may be greater wisdom; our waste may be His wealth. Pain results from the operation of general laws, and must not be interpreted from a narrow and personal viewpoint.

Pain must be considered along with pleasure, and in the light of freedom and the purposes of conscious life. Thus things which are apparently evil, and which *are* evil when viewed singly and from below, can take their place as component parts of a system of good.

APPENDIX I

THE DEDICATION AND THE PREFACE

The Dedication and the Preface of the *Principles*, both of which were omitted from the second edition, contain some points of interest.

It is noteworthy that the two great works, Locke's *Essay* and Berkeley's *Principles*, had the same patron, Thomas, Earl of Pembroke (*b.* 1656, *d.* 1733), who was Lord-Lieutenant of Ireland from April 1707 to November 1708. The *Philosophical Commentaries* has the entry (No. 396), " Engagements to P. on account of ye treatise that grew up under his eye [Locke's *Essay*], on account also of his approving my harangue . . .," from which we may infer that the Earl had been present at a meeting of a College society or of the Dublin Philosophical Society, at which Berkeley had read a paper, perhaps his *Description of the Cave of Dunmore*, or his *Of Infinites*. There are a good many references to the presentation copy of the book in Berkeley's correspondence.[1] When the book at last reached him, Pembroke sent his thanks, saying, " You were an ingenious man and ought to be encouraged, but that he could not be convinced of the non-existence of matter." In London Berkeley made the Earl's acquaintance, and later the two became close friends and correspondents. Pembroke subscribed £300 to the Bermuda enterprise, and advised upon it.[2]

The reference to " our Society " is to Trinity College, Dublin, and "the extraordinary favour and bounty " refers to Pembroke's gift in 1698 of £500 to buy books for the Library, and no doubt also to the Parliamentary grant of £5,000 in 1709 towards erecting a new Library, which Pembroke was probably instrumental in obtaining.

In the Preface the " long and scrupulous inquiry " refers to the close study of the arguments for and against matter represented in the *Philosophical Commentaries*. This work and the *Essay on Vision* and earlier studies probably occupied some four or five years, and it cannot be said that Berkeley rushed into print with a hastily conceived notion. From his letter to Percival of the 6th of September 1710 we know that he deliberately refrained from mentioning the non-existence of matter in the Preface, and the same letter strongly deprecates the charges of " a vain affectation of novelty," and of scepticism about the existence of sensible things.

[1] See Rand, *Berkeley and Percival*, pp. 78, 80, 85-86, 88, 90, 92.
[2] *Ib.* pp. 105, 109, 173 ; Fraser, *Life and Letters*, pp. 107, 170.

APPENDIX II

IMMATERIALISM TO-DAY

A long interval between the conception of " ye immaterial hypothesis " and its general acceptance was to be expected ; for it goes deep. Not quite two hundred years have elapsed since Berkeley died. But what are two hundred years in the history of thought? More than two hundred years, from Thales to Aristotle, were needed to establish the concept of matter ; three hundred years may be needed to break it down. Berkeley was far-sighted, and in many ways he belonged to the nineteenth or the twentieth century. He wanted to give the episcopate to America and to plant the arts and higher learning there ; he wanted a second university in Ireland ; he wanted to admit Roman Catholics to Trinity College without religious disabilities ; he wanted social reform ; he wanted a radical change in political economy ; he attacked the prevailing theory, mercantilism ; he denied that wealth is dead gold in the vaults of the bank, an absolute existent, and he asserted that it is credit and industry, a very relative existent, that, in fact, money is means and therefore in the public mind and common weal and common will. He was not wrong in these other things ; he was before his time ; and when he denied material substance, he was not wrong ; he was before his time.

A century ago T. Collyns Simon challenged the learned world to disprove Berkeley's demonstration of immaterialism or his own " two new demonstrations," or to prove the existence of material substance, offering a prize of one hundred pounds to the essayist who could do one of those three things.[1]

We smile at the notion of establishing truth by the offer of a prize ; but Simon correctly voiced the challenging note in Berkeley's thesis. Simon held that " there is no intermediate position between materialism and immaterialism " (Preface), and that therefore folk ought to make up their minds about it, and decide one way or the other. I quite agree with him there. Berkeley raises a clear-cut issue, presents an attractive case, and once the issue is understood, the thinker can hardly help taking sides. Material substance, like the sea serpent,

[1] Prospectus prefixed to his *On the nature and elements of the external world ; or universal immaterialism fully explained and newly demonstrated*, 1847. In the second edition he triumphantly announces that no essays had been submitted for the prize.

either is or is not ; there are no two ways about it. This is no question about a mere concept or category, or a point of view, or the use of terms ; fundamentally it is a question of fact which calls for an answer, permits an answer, and deserves an answer.

Berkeley's is not " a philosophers' philosophy " ; it has a wide appeal outside the circle of professed metaphysicians. Berkeley said he was willing to be understood by all, and though he has been much misunderstood, he has never been forgotten, and to-day he is more read, or talked about, than ever. He raises questions which rise naturally in the minds of those who think, from their teens upward. What is matter ? Does it exist ? People are not happy about it, and they come to Berkeley for sympathy, if not for satisfaction. They may not agree with him, but they know he is sincere and has something of importance to say. Men of letters, men of science, artists, economists, poets, clergymen, statesmen, and philosophers are in his audience. Not so long ago Bergson said that philosophy must start from Berkeley's problem. John R. Fothergill, one of whose ancestors corresponded with Berkeley, confessed to me recently, apropos the philosophy of art, " Whether the study of Berkeley has helped me or hindered me I cannot say. Anyhow I can't get rid of him now."

We can't get rid of Berkeley now ; but will he make us im-materialists ? I think he will in the end, though perhaps not under that name and style. Few would care to join, in Swift's phrase, " the sect of the immaterialists." The term *immaterialism* is not attractive ; it negates without affirming, destroys without obviously building up, takes away and offers nothing in exchange. But the positive aspects of Berkeley's teaching are making their way slowly and are leavening the lump. Dialectical immaterialism is forcing Berkeley's positive world of sense and his positive world of spirit on the public conscious-ness. There may never be a sudden, dramatic acceptance of im-materialism, such as Simon contemplated ; but when one looks back on the speculative arguments about matter and its relations to God, and to space, and to things, arguments so frequent in the old leather-bound volumes of eighteenth-century philosophy and theology, and taken so seriously then and so lightly now, one can hardly resist the conclusion that the concept of matter has had its day.

We are chary of denying the existence of matter (and there are good reasons for caution and guarded speech), but few take its exist-ence seriously in the laboratory or the lecture room to-day. Matter is becoming more of an adverb and less of a noun ; it is rather a way of thinking than a thing thought. The word has its uses, and it may survive awhile as a collective term for objects of sense or for some of their general features ; in the religious context it may help to safeguard reverence ; in philosophy it comes in handy as a description for *possible* objects of sense when we require to distinguish them from those actually being sensed ; but matter as material substance, matter as an object of speculative faith, matter as the " other " of the sensible world and making two with it, matter as the hidden hand, as the *vera causa* of sensation and of change, such *matter* has no future ; it is the deservedly ridiculed " something we know not what." The euthanasia of material substance cannot be long delayed ; it will die of neglect and disuse, rather than of formal refutation ; for when perceptual analysis has clarified the perceptual situation, and disclosed its two factors, the subject and the object, when the percipient subject is accepted with all its implications and the perceived object is taken at its face value, then material substance just fades out, its occupation gone. Matter puzzles and perplexes us, and explains nothing ; nothing *in rerum natura* corresponds to the term ; no branch of study would be embarrassed by its passing ; thought is quicker and action is surer without it ; a man thinks better, works better, prays better, if he drops it altogether.

I referred in my Preface to W. B. Yeats and his interest in Berkeley, because the poet's mind is here in a measure typical of the public mind. The dry metaphysics of the question did not interest him ; he may, or may not, have been consciously concerned with Berkeley's God ; he was deeply and consciously concerned with Berkeley's world, and that for an obvious reason. Yeats was not content to please with honeyed words ; he was not content to write well about a world of fancy ; he wanted to understand the *real* world and interpret it. He had seen and heard things which he thought were real, but Descartes and Locke and their modern successors cast doubts upon them, saying that what he had seen and heard had only a problematical existence, or did not exist at all, or did not exist as he saw and heard them. The philosophers and the scientists were for taking away the world of the poet and of his public, the world of common sense, and Berkeley had given him back that world. The poet had been made uneasy for the Lake Isle of Innisfree, for its nine bean rows and " the bee-loud glade." He had seen and heard these things, and he knew they were not his private dreams and fancies ; for he could make others see and hear them too. Berkeley had given them all back to him, the song of the cricket, the purple glow, the linnets' wings, and the lake water lapping. Berkeley had brought back " the world that only exists because it shines and sounds," had brought it back certified real and existing, because *esse est percipi*. Now Yeats can write freely about the sights he sees and the sounds he hears, assured that in making beauty he is not making believe, or saying sweet things about the non-existent. Now he need not go, cap in hand, to the science of matter, and ask if he might mention the glimmer of midnight, and low sounds by the shore. For the glimmer and the murmur are " perfectly known, there being nothing in them which is not perceived " [1] The poet is now like Hylas, when Philonous has converted him, and Hylas exclaims, " I have been a long time distrusting my senses ; me thought I saw things by a dim light and through false glasses. Now the glasses are removed, and a new light breaks in on my understanding. I am clearly convinced that I see things in their native forms, and am no longer in pain about their unknown natures or absolute existence." [2] Matter, says Berkeley, is " the very root of scepticism " [3] and because men are tired of scepticism and semi-scepticism, and with the poet seek assurance about their environment, they turn to Berkeley and find that his denial of matter is an assertion of the sensible world, giving assurance of its existence and of our direct contact with it.

In the philosophical world to-day there is a good deal of silent sympathy with immaterialism, but plain statements on the question are few, and plain avowals of immaterialism are fewer. Our professors, for the most part, assume the traditional account of matter, but say little about it ; we are very naturally afraid (for it is a thorny subject) of being misunderstood by our scientific colleagues and the general public. Some confess that in their youth, like Thomas Reid, they toyed awhile with Berkeley, adding that in later life they have seen the error of those ways. Some appear to compromise, and compound, as it were, with Berkeley. They give up matter, but keep " the physical object," distinguishing it from the datum of sense. Some, like jugglers, try to keep the three balls in the air at once, defending matter and the physical object and the sense datum. But *entia non sunt multiplicanda*. Given sense data what more in that line is required ? What more can be fitted in ? Analysis of man's concrete perceptual situation yields the percipient subject, the perceived object, and nothing more. The contemporary movement of thought that has compelled us all to take seriously and objectively the first

---

[1] *Princ.*, 87 ; see above, pp. 135–36.
[2] *Three Dialogues*, iii. *ad fin.*
[3] *Princ.*, 86 ; see above, pp. 135–36.

things in sense perception (whether we call them sensa, or sense data, or sensations, or phenomena, or appearances, or, with Berkeley, ideas), compels us to reject all other non-spiritual objects. By fine-spun distinctions between the perceived and the perceivable, and between the group and its components, we may make a case for retaining the names *matter* and *the physical object* side by side with the sense datum ; but ultimately these other entities merge in the object of sense or sink to the level of intellectual constructs.

The realist movement, the revolt from representationism, and the spread of " the regularity view " of physical causation have told strongly in Berkeley's favour. The universal nexus of physical causes, dear to Victorian philosophers, has gone, and its place is taken by a view indistinguishable from Berkeley's customary con-nection of sign and thing signified. The multiplicity of little material causes is being replaced by the one great spiritual Cause. Matter can hardly survive the passing of the material cause. The constant " sum total of matter " which used to bestride the world of philo-sophical thought " like a Colossus," has dwindled to the stature of a heuristic principle, a form of the logical law that A is A, and is not not-A.

The most stubborn defence of matter will be found in religious circles ; but there it is the name *matter* that is defended, rather than the thing. A sharp division of religious opinion is here inevitable, and perhaps salutary ; for it represents the tension between theory and practice. Religion has to train men to be religious, not simply to accept the truth ; it must teach " here a little and there a little," and must therefore make verbal concessions, and be content to use imperfect statements and provisional truths. Religious minds who feel keenly the attraction of Berkeley's teaching see clearly the great practical difficulties in applying it ; among the clergy immaterialism makes slow headway. Conservative theologians usually think of matter as an intermediate creation. God first created matter, they think, and out of it made the ordered world, or allowed " evolution " to do so. The parish priest who is not much concerned with cos-mogony, but is in daily contact with the human soul, finds something almost shocking in Berkeley's approach to the infinite. Not by accident does the Berkeley memorial window in the Chapel of his College bear the text, " When the multitude heard, they were astonished at his doctrine." The doctrines of the immediate presence and direct operation of God are " strong meat," and when he hears Berkeley say that we have only to open our eyes to see " manifest tokens of the Divinity," the parson feels suspicious. This makes belief too easy. *Credo quia absurdum.* Where is the merit of believing in spirit, if its existence is so obvious ? Where is its moral value, if belief is so effortless ? Has not Berkeley torn down a screen between God and man—a screen which in the interests of reverence and piety ought to stand ? In theory God is in the market-place as well as in the church ; but the sacred is not the profane, and we must have fences if religion is to flourish. In theory God works all, in all ; but can we bring ourselves to admit that the divine power which forgives sins boils the breakfast egg ? Berkeley has answered these difficulties [1] but only philosophers can fully appreciate his answers, and, unfortunately, religion and philosophy are not very willing to learn from one another to-day. Truth is truth, however, and if it is philosophically true that there is neither matter nor operative " nature " other than spirit, then any use of such terms and notions in religion is only a verbal concession to practice, and has no metaphysical basis.

If the scientific attitude to matter be fairly reflected in the pages of the *Encyclopedia Britannica*, as one would expect it to be, then modern science has lost, or is losing, interest in matter as an absolute existent out of mind, and retains the term merely as a general description for things sensible, or for those aspects and features of them which matter most for counting and calculation. The *Encyclopedia* (14th edition) contains no *ad hoc* article on matter, and under MATTER it simply gives the reference, " see Kinetic Theory of Matter ; Atom ; Nucleus." In those highly technical and specialist articles there is little mention of matter as such, and where the term does occur, sensible objects, solid, liquid, or gaseous, could be substituted for it without alteration of meaning. No reader would gather from those articles that science to-day had any living interest in the historic concept, or that material substance entered in any way into laboratory work or into any scientific speculations reasonably founded thereon. And if we are to equate material substance with the sensible, or with those features of the sensible which are of importance to us all, then we reach the paradoxical results that this absolute existent is extremely relative, and that matter is what everybody minds.

Some say that true-blue material substance does play a part in theoretical physics, because the constituent is there regarded as being of a different nature from the thing constituted. On this showing the sensible thing we see and touch would have material constituents which cannot be seen and touched ; sensible lithium, for instance, would not rank as matter, and the matter of the lithium would be the atoms, nuclei, electrons, etc., which compose it. But science

[1] See *Princ.*, 51–53, 75, 106–7, 117, 150–56 ; *Three Dialogues*, iii.

is not communicative on this topic, or clear. It is very doubtful whether science does hold any such view, or could do so ; we can hardly think of the sensible as being composed of the absolutely non-sensible ; we can hardly think of the sub-microscopic as being of a totally different kind from the microscopic and the macroscopic ; we can hardly think that there are two objective worlds differing fundamentally in kind, the one composed of the things we touch and see, and the other composed of electrons in their courses. I have heard a physicist say outright that atoms, electrons, etc., are like symbols in algebra, and that to ask whether they exist is a futile thing, like asking whether x and y in an algebraical formula exist. That may, or may not, be the accepted theory of modern physics ; but in either case, it seems obvious that a laboratory experiment, however far-reaching its conclusions, starts from objects of sense, ends with objects of sense, and establishes facts about objects of sense, working throughout by reasoning based on perceptions of sense. And, if that be so, can we regard the concepts of sub-atomic physics as constituting matter, in any sense of the term *matter* not applicable also to the things we touch and see ? [1]

Sir James Jeans would be inclined, I think, to answer, No. In his *Physics and Philosophy* (1942, p. 216) he says that the concept of matter needs to be drastically revised, and he uses the striking phrase " the ghostly remains of matter." He is deliberately summing up, writing with care and caution, and weighing his words. His " the ghostly remains of matter " is reminiscent of Berkeley's " the ghosts of departed quantities " (*Analyst*, 35), and Jeans' use of the phrase almost necessarily implies, I think, that he regards the historic concept of material substance as, from the standpoint of science, virtually dead. Here is the passage :

" We cannot state any positive conclusion of any kind, as for instance that materialism is dead, or that a deterministic interpretation of the world is obsolete, but we can say that determinism and freedom, matter and materialism, need to be re-defined in the light of our new scientific knowledge. When this has been done, the materialist must decide for himself, whether the only kind of materialism which science now permits can be suitably labelled materialism,

---

[1] Since the above was written, public attention has been called to the atom by developments of physics of serious concern to all. The " atomic " bomb painfully, it seems to me, bears out the truth of the argument of this paragraph. It explodes the " big box " theory of the universe and the " little box " theory of things, and shows that the things of sense are sensible through and through.

and whether the ghostly remains of matter should be labelled as matter, or as something else. It is merely a question of terminology.

" What remains is in any case very different from the full-blooded matter and the forbidding materialism of the Victorian scientist. His objective and material universe is proved to consist of little more than constructs of our own minds. In this and in other ways modern physics has moved in the direction of mentalism."

What Jeans here calls " mentalism " is more exactly, I think, called immaterialism.